NEW YORK TEST PREP

Practice Test Book

Next Gen Mathematics

Grade 3

ISBN 9798566183312

TEST MASTER PRESS

CONTENTS

INTRODUCTION
For Parents, Teachers, and Tutors

About the New York Mathematics Tests

Students in New York will be assessed by taking the New York State Mathematics tests. This practice workbook will prepare students for the tests. It contains four warm-up practice sets that will introduce students to the tests. This is followed by practice sets that provide specific practice with the types of questions found on the test.

Warm-Up Sets

The warm-up sets are short tests that will introduce students to the tests and give them practice before taking the full-length practice sets. They include the types of questions students will encounter on the real tests, with a strong focus on more rigorous short-response and extended-response questions. The first two tests contains 10 questions each and the second two tests contain 20 questions each.

Practice Sets

The mini-tests are followed by full-length practice sets that are similar to the test sessions that students complete on the real tests. On the real tests, students answer multiple-choice questions and written answer questions. This includes short-response and extended-response questions. These written answer questions require students to complete complex tasks and may require students to explain their thinking or show their work. This practice test book provides complete sets of written answer questions and includes more questions than are found on the real tests. The additional short-response and extended-response questions will ensure that all the skills are covered and will give students more practice applying skills and answering complex questions.

Calculators and Tools

Students should be provided with a ruler to use on all parts of the test. Students are not allowed to use a calculator on any part of the tests, and so should complete all the practice tests without the use of a calculator.

About the Next Generation Learning Standards

In 2017, the state of New York introduced the Next Generation Learning Standards. These are revised standards that replace the previous Common Core Learning Standards, though remain very close in content. Beginning with the 2020/2021 school year, the state tests will assess the Next Generation Learning Standards. This practice test book aligns all questions to the Next Generation Learning Standards.

New York Mathematics

Practice Set 1

Mixed Questions

Instructions

Read each question carefully. For each multiple-choice question, fill in the circle for the correct answer. For other types of questions, follow the directions given in the question.

You may use a ruler to help you answer questions. You may not use a calculator on this test.

---

1   Which fraction is represented by point *Y*?

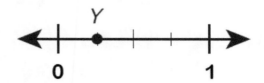

Ⓐ $\dfrac{1}{3}$

Ⓑ $\dfrac{1}{4}$

Ⓒ $\dfrac{1}{5}$

Ⓓ $\dfrac{1}{8}$

2   Sandra started walking to school at 8:45 a.m. It took her 25 minutes to get to school. What time did she get to school?

Ⓐ   9:00 a.m.

Ⓑ   9:10 a.m.

Ⓒ   9:15 a.m.

Ⓓ   9:20 a.m.

3   Karisa wants to determine how much water the dog bowl below can hold. Which measurement would Karisa be best to find?

   Ⓐ   Volume

   Ⓑ   Weight

   Ⓒ   Height

   Ⓓ   Length

4   Morgan earns money on the weekend by washing cars. He washed 4 cars for $8 each. He was also given a tip of $5 by one customer. How much money did Morgan make in all? Write an expression below to show how much Morgan made, in dollars. Then simplify the expression to find how much Morgan made, in dollars.

Expression _____

Answer _____

5 Select **all** the equations that will be true if the number 8 is placed in the empty box.

☐ $6 \times \boxed{} = 48$

☐ $8 \times \boxed{} = 56$

☐ $9 \times \boxed{} = 72$

☐ $24 \div \boxed{} = 4$

☐ $40 \div \boxed{} = 5$

☐ $64 \div \boxed{} = 8$

6 Plot the four fractions listed below on the number line.

$$\frac{3}{4} \qquad \frac{6}{3} \qquad \frac{4}{4} \qquad \frac{3}{1}$$

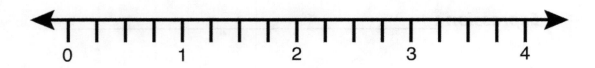

7 Sam kept a record of the types of movies each customer in his store rented. Sam made the table below to show the results.

Type of Movie	Number of Rentals
Action	12
Comedy	14
Drama	8
Science fiction	18

Use the information in the table to complete the graph below.

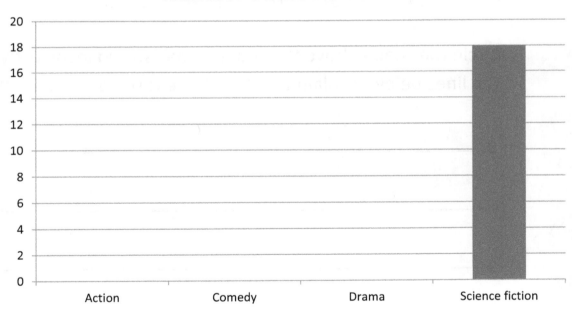

8 Hannah sorts the figures below into those that are parallelograms and those that are not parallelograms.

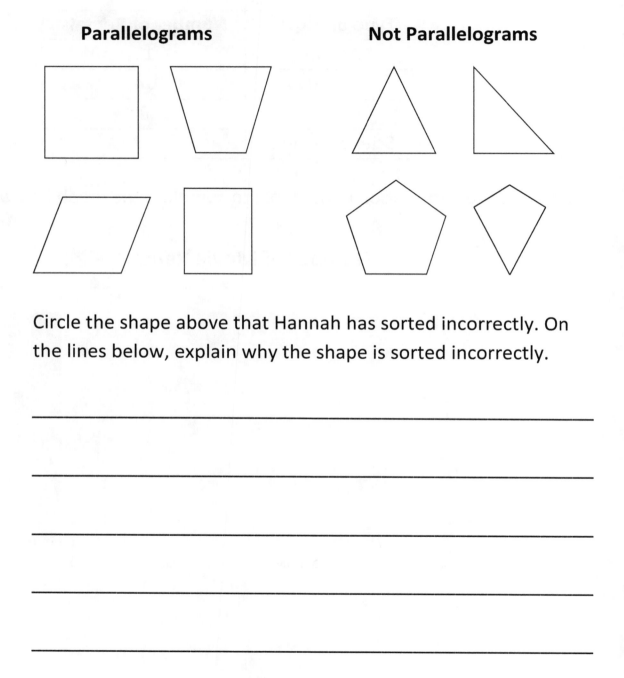

Circle the shape above that Hannah has sorted incorrectly. On the lines below, explain why the shape is sorted incorrectly.

_____

_____

_____

_____

_____

9   Emilio wants to create a vegetable garden with the shape shown below. On the diagram below, write the numbers in the boxes to show the missing dimensions.

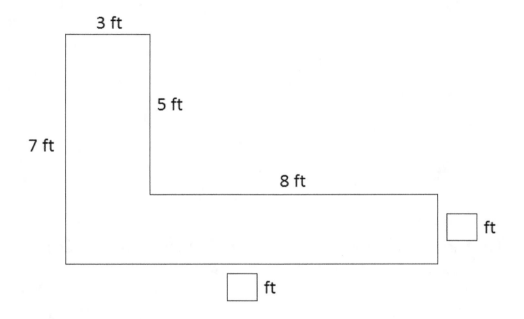

Draw a line on the diagram to divide it into two rectangles. Find the total area of the garden. Write your answer below.

_____ square feet

Find the perimeter of the garden. Write your answer below.

_____ feet

10 Craig draws the rectangle below. Craig states that all rectangles with an area of 12 square units have a perimeter of 14 units. On the grid above, draw a second rectangle that shows that Craig is incorrect.

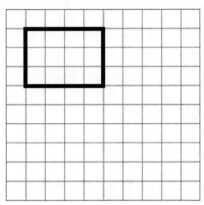

On the lines below, explain how you can tell that Craig is incorrect.

_____

_____

_____

_____

_____

END OF PRACTICE SET

New York Mathematics

Practice Set 2

Mixed Questions

Instructions

Read each question carefully. For each multiple-choice question, fill in the circle for the correct answer. For other types of questions, follow the directions given in the question.

You may use a ruler to help you answer questions. You may not use a calculator on this test.

1   Ryan's basketball team scored 74 points in a match. The team won the match by 9 points. How many points did the other team score?

Ⓐ   81

Ⓑ   83

Ⓒ   65

Ⓓ   67

2   Andy is learning to speak French. Andy learns 5 new words every day. Complete the table below to show how many words Andy has learned in all after each day.

Number of Days	Number of Words Learned
1	
2	
3	
4	
5	

3   Anton looked at the clock below.

Which of the following is closest to the time shown on the clock?

Ⓐ   6:20

Ⓑ   4:30

Ⓒ   4:45

Ⓓ   9:00

4   What is the length of the nail shown below? Write your answer below.

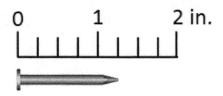

_____ inches

5 Select **all** the fractions that are equivalent to the shaded area of the circle below.

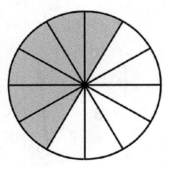

☐ $\dfrac{6}{1}$

☐ $\dfrac{1}{2}$

☐ $\dfrac{6}{12}$

☐ $\dfrac{2}{4}$

☐ $\dfrac{8}{4}$

☐ $\dfrac{2}{3}$

6 Jo has 18 star-shaped stickers. He places them in 3 even rows. Which of these shows how many stickers are in each row?

Ⓐ

Ⓑ

Ⓒ

Ⓓ

7 Simon had $896 in his savings account. He spent $179 on car repairs. How much money does Simon have left? Write your answer below.

$ _____

8   Alex started the number pattern below. Continue the pattern by writing the next four numbers on the lines below.

6, 10, 14, 18, 22, _____, _____, _____, _____

Will all the numbers in the pattern be even? Explain why or why not.

_____

_____

_____

_____

_____

9 The pictograph below shows how long Tammy spent at the computer each week day.

Monday	🖥🖥🖥🖥
Tuesday	🖥🖥🖥🖥🖥🖥
Wednesday	🖥🖥🖥🖥🖥
Thursday	🖥🖥🖥
Friday	🖥🖥

Each 🖥 means 10 minutes.

On which day did Tammy spend the least time at the computer? Write your answer below.

_____

How many minutes did Tammy spend at the computer on Monday? Write your answer below.

_____ minutes

How much more time did Tammy spend at the computer on Tuesday than Thursday? Write your answer below.

_____ minutes

10   Look at the shaded figure below.

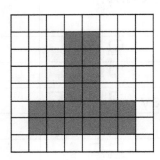

Divide the figure into two rectangles. Write the dimensions of the two rectangles below.

Rectangle 1: _____ by _____ units

Rectangle 2: _____ by _____ units

What is the total area of the shaded figure? Write your answer below.

_____ square units

END OF PRACTICE SET

New York Mathematics

Practice Set 3

Mixed Questions

Instructions

Read each question carefully. For each multiple-choice question, fill in the circle for the correct answer. For other types of questions, follow the directions given in the question.

You may use a ruler to help you answer questions. You may not use a calculator on this test.

---

1 Mario buys screws in packets of 6.

If Mario counts the screws in groups of 6, which of these numbers would he count?

Ⓐ   20

Ⓑ   24

Ⓒ   28

Ⓓ   32

2 The graph shows how long Jason studied for one week.

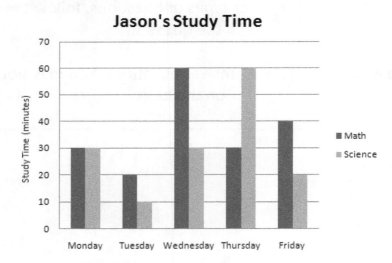

On what day did Jason study science for 30 minutes less than math? Write your answer below.

_____

3 Which fraction below is equal to 4?

Ⓐ $\dfrac{2}{8}$

Ⓑ $\dfrac{8}{4}$

Ⓒ $\dfrac{15}{5}$

Ⓓ $\dfrac{12}{3}$

4 Sally is making a pictograph to show how many students are in grade 3, grade 4, and grade 5.

Grade 3	☺☺☺☺☺☺☺☺☺☺☺
Grade 4	☺☺☺☺☺☺☺☺☺☺☺☺☺
Grade 5	

☺ = 5 students

There are 65 students in grade 5. Which of these should Sally use to represent 65 students?

Ⓐ ☺☺☺☺☺☺☺☺☺☺☺

Ⓑ ☺☺☺☺☺☺☺☺☺☺☺☺

Ⓒ ☺☺☺☺☺☺☺☺☺☺☺☺☺

Ⓓ ☺☺☺☺☺☺☺☺☺☺☺☺☺☺

5   Damon rode 3 miles to school every morning, and 3 miles back home each afternoon. How many miles would he ride in 5 days?

Ⓐ   15 miles

Ⓑ   30 miles

Ⓒ   45 miles

Ⓓ   60 miles

6   Ribbon costs $4 per yard. Allie buys 16 yards of ribbon. Which number sentence could be used to find the total cost of the ribbon, c, in dollars?

Ⓐ $16 + 4 = c$

Ⓑ $16 - 4 = c$

Ⓒ $16 \times 4 = c$

Ⓓ $16 \div 4 = c$

7   Allen's car has traveled 25,648 miles since it was new. What is this number rounded to the nearest hundred? Write your answer below.

_____

8 The school library has 1,532 fiction books, 1,609 non-fiction books, and 1,239 children's books. Which number sentence shows the best way to estimate the total number of books?

Ⓐ   1,500 + 1,600 + 1,200 = 4,300

Ⓑ   1,500 + 1,600 + 1,300 = 4,400

Ⓒ   1,600 + 1,600 + 1,300 = 4,500

Ⓓ   1,600 + 1,700 + 1,300 = 4,600

9 There are 157 male students and 165 female students at Ella's school. How many students are there in all?

Ⓐ   322

Ⓑ   312

Ⓒ   222

Ⓓ   212

10 Plot the fraction $1\frac{1}{4}$ on the number line below.

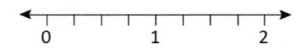

11 Look at the group of numbers below. Round each number to the nearest ten. Write your answers below.

108 _____   864 _____

87 _____   196 _____

282 _____   35 _____

981 _____   773 _____

On the lines below, explain how you decided whether to round each number up or down.

_____

_____

_____

_____

12   During the baseball season, Marvin's team won 5 games and lost 14 games.

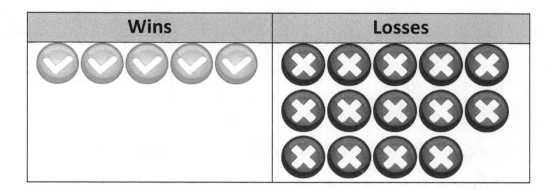

What fraction of the total games did the team win?

Show your work.

Answer _____

13 Shade the models below to show $\frac{3}{10}$ and $\frac{1}{5}$.

 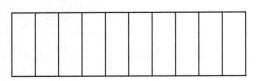

Place one of the symbols below in the number sentence to compare the fractions $\frac{3}{10}$ and $\frac{1}{5}$.

$$<, >, =$$

$\frac{3}{10}$ ☐ $\frac{1}{5}$

On the lines below, explain how the models helped you find the answer.

_____

_____

_____

_____

14   Look at the pattern below.

$$16, 19, 22, 25, 28, 31, \underline{\hspace{1.5cm}}$$

Write an expression that can be used to find the next number in the pattern. Use x to represent the last number in the pattern.

Expression _____

Use the expression to find the next number in the pattern.

Answer _____

Use the expression to find the number that would come after 112.

Answer _____

15 Complete the number sentences below to show **three** different ways to complete the calculation in two steps.

$$6 \times 5 \times 3$$

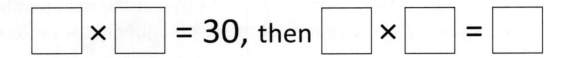

☐ × ☐ = 30, then ☐ × ☐ = ☐

☐ × ☐ = 18, then ☐ × ☐ = ☐

☐ × ☐ = 15, then ☐ × ☐ = ☐

16 A company has 8 salespersons. Each salesperson works about 40 hours each week. About how many hours do all the salespeople work in all?

Ⓐ   32

Ⓑ   48

Ⓒ   320

Ⓓ   480

17 A dance class usually has 30 students in it. On Monday, there were 6 students missing from the class and 2 extra students visiting the class. Write the correct symbols in the boxes to complete the number sentence that shows how many students were in the class on Monday. Then complete the calculation.

$$30 \;\square\; 6 \;\square\; 2 = \square$$

18 There were 17,856 people living in Eastwood in 2009. What is the value of the digit 8 in 17,856?

Ⓐ Eight hundred

Ⓑ Eight thousand

Ⓒ Eighty thousand

Ⓓ Eighty

19   What fraction of the model is shaded?

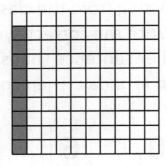

Ⓐ $\frac{1}{9}$

Ⓑ $\frac{9}{10}$

Ⓒ $\frac{9}{91}$

Ⓓ $\frac{9}{100}$

20   Which of the following is another way to write quarter past five?

Ⓐ   5:25

Ⓑ   5:30

Ⓒ   5:45

Ⓓ   5:15

END OF PRACTICE SET

New York Mathematics

Practice Set 4

Mixed Questions

Instructions

Read each question carefully. For each multiple-choice question, fill in the circle for the correct answer. For other types of questions, follow the directions given in the question.

You may use a ruler to help you answer questions. You may not use a calculator on this test.

---

1   Which of these shows one way to divide a hexagon into two parts with equal areas?

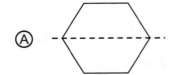

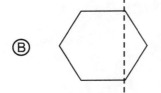

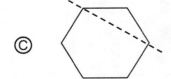

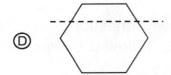

2   There were some people on a bus. After a stop, there were 4 times as many people on the bus. If there were 36 people on the bus after the stop, which equation can be used to find how many people, *p*, were on the bus to start with?

Ⓐ $p \times 4 = 36$

Ⓑ $p \div 4 = 36$

Ⓒ $p + 4 = 36$

Ⓓ $p - 4 = 36$

3   Inga made the design below.

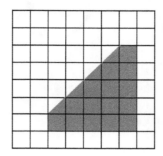

Each square measures 1 square centimeter. What is the area of the shaded part of the design?

Ⓐ   16 square centimeters

Ⓑ   17 square centimeters

Ⓒ   18 square centimeters

Ⓓ   19 square centimeters

4   Which statement describes both a trapezoid and a rectangle?

Ⓐ   It is a quadrilateral.

Ⓑ   It has four equal angles.

Ⓒ   It is a parallelogram.

Ⓓ   It has two pairs of perpendicular sides.

5   What is the best estimate of the mass of a lemon?

Ⓐ   2 grams

Ⓑ   200 grams

Ⓒ   2 kilograms

Ⓓ   200 kilograms

6   Look at the number pattern below.

48, 42, 36, 30, 24, ...

If the pattern continues, what two numbers will come next?

Ⓐ   22, 20

Ⓑ   30, 36

Ⓒ   20, 16

Ⓓ   18, 12

7 Rita made the pictograph below to show how many cans each class collected for a food drive.

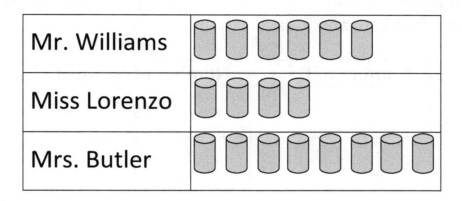

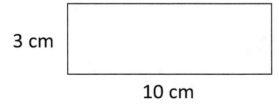 = 4 cans

How many cans did Miss Lorenzo's class collect? Write your answer below.

_____ cans

8 What is the perimeter of the rectangle below?

3 cm ▢

10 cm

Ⓐ 13 cm

Ⓑ 30 cm

Ⓒ 26 cm

Ⓓ 60 cm

9 Lei jogs for the same number of minutes every day. The table shows how far she jogs in total after 1, 2, 3, and 4 days. Complete the table to show how many minutes Lei jogs for in total after 5, 6, and 7 days.

Number of Days	Number of Minutes
1	15
2	30
3	45
4	60
5	
6	
7	

10   The table below shows how many coins of each type Joshua has.

Coin	Number of Coins
Penny	9
Nickel	4
Dime	5
Quarter	2

What fraction of the coins are quarters?

Ⓐ $\dfrac{1}{2}$

Ⓑ $\dfrac{1}{4}$

Ⓒ $\dfrac{1}{10}$

Ⓓ $\dfrac{1}{20}$

11 Round 8,782 to the nearest ten and the nearest hundred. Write your answers on the lines below.

Nearest ten _____

Nearest hundred _____

On the lines below, explain how you worked out whether to round the number up or down in each case.

_____

_____

_____

_____

_____

12   Harris saved $96 in 16 weeks. He saved the same amount of money each week. How much did Harris save each week?

Show your work.

Answer $_____

13   Joy got on a train at 1:35 p.m. Joy got off the train at 3:06 p.m. For how many minutes was Joy on the train?

Show your work.

Answer _____ minutes

14 Shade the fractions $\frac{1}{2}$ and $\frac{2}{4}$ on the fraction models below.

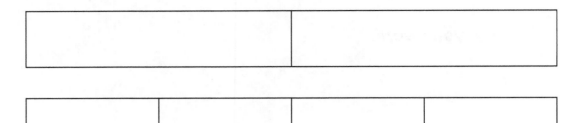

Shade the fraction model below to show another fraction equivalent to $\frac{1}{2}$ and $\frac{2}{4}$. Write the fraction on the line below.

Fraction _____

15 What is the area of the rectangle shown on the grid below? Write your answer below.

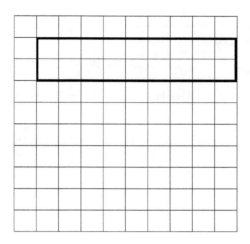

_____ square units

On the grid below, draw a rectangle with the same area but a different perimeter.

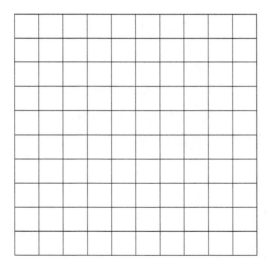

16 Margaret surveyed students about who they would vote for in a class election. Davis made the graph below to show the results.

Davis	☺☺☺☺
Bobby	
Inga	☺☺☺☺☺☺☺

Each ☺ means 2 students.

In the survey, 8 students said they would vote for Bobby. How many symbols should Margaret use to show 8 votes?

Ⓐ   8

Ⓑ   4

Ⓒ   2

Ⓓ   16

17 Kim is 63 inches tall. Chelsea is 4 inches taller than Kim. Vicky is 3 inches shorter than Chelsea. Which expression could be used to find Vicky's height, in inches?

Ⓐ $63 - 4 - 3$

Ⓑ $63 + 4 + 3$

Ⓒ $63 - 4 + 3$

Ⓓ $63 + 4 - 3$

18 Miss Jenkins received wages of $655. She saved $80 of her wages and spent the rest. How much money did Miss Jenkins spend? Write your answer below.

$ _____

19 Bananas sell for $3 per pound. Stacey buys 9 pounds of bananas. How much would the bananas cost?

Ⓐ $12

Ⓑ $27

Ⓒ $18

Ⓓ $21

20 A picture frame is 8 inches wide and 5 inches high. What is the perimeter of the frame?

Ⓐ 26 inches

Ⓑ 32 inches

Ⓒ 20 inches

Ⓓ 40 inches

END OF PRACTICE SET

New York Mathematics

Practice Set 5

Multiple-Choice Questions

Instructions

Read each question carefully. For each multiple-choice question, fill in the circle for the correct answer.

You may use a ruler to help you answer questions. You may not use a calculator on this test.

---

1 Sara walked around the four outside edges of a football field. If Sara recorded the total distance she walked, what would Sara have determined?

    Ⓐ   The area of the football field

    Ⓑ   The volume of the football field

    Ⓒ   The perimeter of the football field

    Ⓓ   The surface area of the football field

2 A piece of note paper has side lengths of 12 centimeters. What is the area of the piece of note paper?

    Ⓐ   48 square centimeters

    Ⓑ   72 square centimeters

    Ⓒ   120 square centimeters

    Ⓓ   144 square centimeters

3 Leah made 500 cakes of soap to sell at a fair. She sold 218 cakes of soap on Saturday. Then she sold 182 cakes of soap on Sunday. Which expression can be used to find how many cakes of soap she had left?

Ⓐ   500 − (218 + 182)

Ⓑ   500 − (218 − 182)

Ⓒ   500 + (218 − 182)

Ⓓ   500 + (218 + 182)

4 Michael drove 1,285 miles during a vacation. How far did Michael drive to the nearest hundred and the nearest ten?

Ⓐ   1,200 miles and 1,280 miles

Ⓑ   1,200 miles and 1,290 miles

Ⓒ   1,300 miles and 1,280 miles

Ⓓ   1,300 miles and 1,290 miles

5 Donna has 18 roses. She wants to put the roses into vases so that each vase has the same number of roses, with no roses left over.

How many roses could Donna put in each vase?

Ⓐ   4

Ⓑ   5

Ⓒ   6

Ⓓ   8

6 Patrick bought 2 packets of 8 pencils for $4 per packet. He also bought 3 packets of 5 crayons for $3 per packet. How much did Patrick spend in all?

Ⓐ $17

Ⓑ $25

Ⓒ $47

Ⓓ $64

7   Look at the shaded figure below.

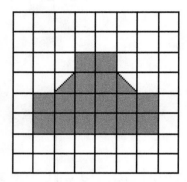

What is the area of the shaded figure?

Ⓐ   17 square units

Ⓑ   16 square units

Ⓒ   18 square units

Ⓓ   24 square units

8   Billy collects pennies and nickels. Billy has 142 pennies and 56 nickels in his coin collection. Which is the best estimate of the total number of coins in Billy's collection?

Ⓐ   150

Ⓑ   180

Ⓒ   200

Ⓓ   250

9 The figure below models the number sentence 6 × 2 = 12.

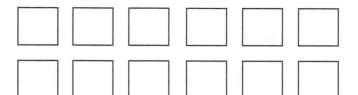

Which number sentence is modeled by the same figure?

Ⓐ 6 ÷ 2 = 3

Ⓑ 36 ÷ 3 = 12

Ⓒ 12 ÷ 6 = 2

Ⓓ 24 ÷ 2 = 12

10 Which numbers make the number sentences below true?

$$8 \times \boxed{} = 8 \qquad 8 \times \boxed{} = 0$$

Ⓐ 1 and 0

Ⓑ 1 and $\frac{1}{8}$

Ⓒ 0 and 8

Ⓓ $\frac{1}{8}$ and 0

11 The graph shows how far four students travel to school.

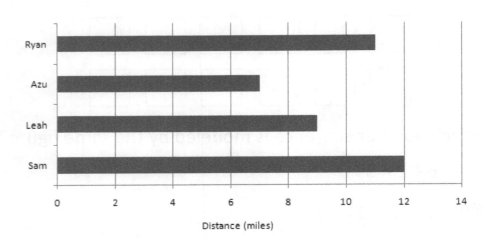

Distance (miles)

How much farther does Ryan travel than Azu?

Ⓐ   4 miles

Ⓑ   6 miles

Ⓒ   11 miles

Ⓓ   18 miles

12 What is the total area of the shaded portion of the grid?

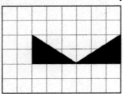

Ⓐ   3 square units

Ⓑ   6 square units

Ⓒ   12 square units

Ⓓ   16 square units

13 A school play was performed on three nights. The table below shows the number of people that saw the school play each night.

Day	Number of People
Friday	225
Saturday	318
Sunday	290

Which number sentence shows the best estimate of the total number of people who saw the school play?

Ⓐ   200 + 300 + 200 = 700

Ⓑ   200 + 300 + 300 = 800

Ⓒ   200 + 400 + 300 = 900

Ⓓ   300 + 400 + 300 = 1,000

14 What fraction of the coins below are quarters?

Ⓐ $\dfrac{1}{2}$

Ⓑ $\dfrac{1}{3}$

Ⓒ $\dfrac{2}{3}$

Ⓓ $\dfrac{3}{5}$

15   Which number sentence represents the array shown below?

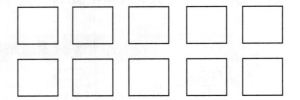

Ⓐ   5 + 2 = 7

Ⓑ   5 × 5 = 25

Ⓒ   5 × 2 = 10

Ⓓ   5 − 2 = 3

16   Which fraction is plotted on the number line below?

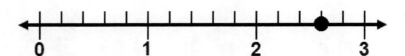

Ⓐ $2\frac{1}{2}$

Ⓑ $2\frac{3}{4}$

Ⓒ $2\frac{2}{3}$

Ⓓ $2\frac{3}{5}$

17   The table below shows the different colors of marbles in a bag.

Color	Number of Marbles
Red	5
Green	10
Blue	2
White	3

Which color makes up $\frac{1}{4}$ of the marbles?

Ⓐ   Red

Ⓑ   Green

Ⓒ   Blue

Ⓓ   White

18   Leah has 3 pies. She cut each pie into eighths.

How many pieces of pie does Leah have?

Ⓐ   24

Ⓑ   16

Ⓒ   18

Ⓓ   32

19 Sarah needs a screwdriver that is smaller than $\frac{3}{8}$ inch. Which screwdriver size is less than $\frac{3}{8}$ inch?

Ⓐ $\frac{1}{2}$ inch

Ⓑ $\frac{3}{4}$ inch

Ⓒ $\frac{1}{4}$ inch

Ⓓ $\frac{5}{8}$ inch

20 A gift card has a length of 150 mm and a width of 50 mm. What is the perimeter of the gift card?

Ⓐ 200 mm

Ⓑ 400 mm

Ⓒ 600 mm

Ⓓ 800 mm

21 Which of these shapes can be divided into two equal triangles by drawing a vertical line down the center?

Ⓐ
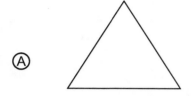

Ⓑ
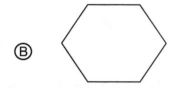

Ⓒ
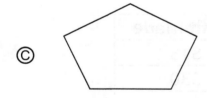

Ⓓ
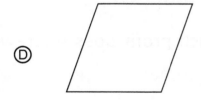

22 Kym is going camping. It costs $16 per night for the campsite. Kym plans to stay for 12 nights. How much will the campsite cost for 12 nights?

Ⓐ $82

Ⓑ $144

Ⓒ $168

Ⓓ $192

23 Andrew is selling muffins at a bake sale. The table shows the profit he makes by selling 5, 10, 15, and 20 muffins.

Muffins Sold	Profit Made
5	$15
10	$30
15	$45
20	$60

Based on the table above, how much profit does Andrew make for selling 1 muffin?

Ⓐ $15

Ⓑ $5

Ⓒ $3

Ⓓ $2

24   What is the area of the square below?

6 cm

Ⓐ   12 cm²

Ⓑ   24 cm²

Ⓒ   36 cm²

Ⓓ   48 cm²

25   Mrs. Bowen cooked dinner for 24 guests. She cooked 3 courses for each guest. Which equation shows how many courses Mrs. Bowen cooked, c?

Ⓐ $24 \times 3 = c$

Ⓑ $24 + 3 = c$

Ⓒ $24 - 3 = c$

Ⓓ $24 \div 3 = c$

26   Danika's flight was expected to depart at 11:55 a.m. Danika's flight left 20 minutes later than expected. What time did Danika's flight depart?

    Ⓐ   11:35 a.m.

    Ⓑ   12:05 p.m.

    Ⓒ   12:15 p.m.

    Ⓓ   12:25 p.m.

27   Which expression is another way to show 12×2?

    Ⓐ $(4 + 3) \times 2$

    Ⓑ $(4 \times 3) \times 2$

    Ⓒ $(4 + 3) + 2$

    Ⓓ $(4 \times 3) + 2$

28   What number makes the equation below true?

$$6 = \underline{} \div 7$$

    Ⓐ   13

    Ⓑ   26

    Ⓒ   42

    Ⓓ   48

29   Abi filled measuring jugs with water and milk, as shown below.

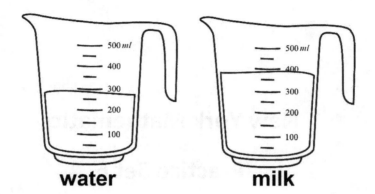

Abi poured the water and milk into a mixing bowl. What volume of liquid would be in the mixing bowl?

Ⓐ   500 ml

Ⓑ   600 ml

Ⓒ   700 ml

Ⓓ   800 ml

30   The Brooklyn Bridge is 1,825 meters long. What is 1,825 rounded to the nearest ten?

Ⓐ   1,800

Ⓑ   1,900

Ⓒ   1,820

Ⓓ   1,830

END OF PRACTICE SET

New York Mathematics

Practice Set 6

Multiple-Choice Questions

Instructions
Read each question carefully. For each multiple-choice question, fill in the circle for the correct answer.
You may use a ruler to help you answer questions. You may not use a calculator on this test.

1 Which number is 3 more than the product of 4 and 23?

Ⓐ 80

Ⓑ 89

Ⓒ 92

Ⓓ 95

2 The graph below shows the high temperature in Dallas for five days.

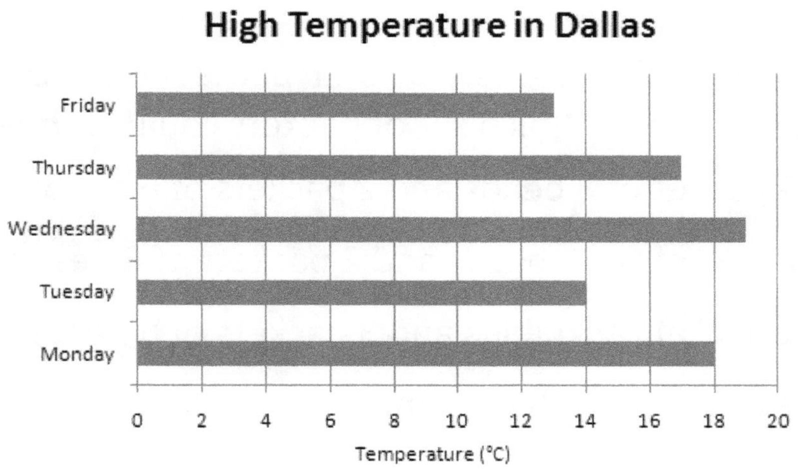

High Temperature in Dallas

On which day was the high temperature 5°C less than the day with the highest temperature?

Ⓐ Monday

Ⓑ Tuesday

Ⓒ Thursday

Ⓓ Friday

3 Which model is shaded to show a fraction equivalent to $\frac{6}{8}$?

Ⓐ

Ⓑ

Ⓒ

Ⓓ

4 Beads are sold in packets of 6 or packets of 8. Liz needs to buy exactly 30 beads. Which set of packets could Liz buy?

Ⓐ   1 packet of 8 beads and 2 packets of 6 beads

Ⓑ   2 packets of 8 beads and 2 packets of 6 beads

Ⓒ   1 packet of 8 beads and 3 packets of 6 beads

Ⓓ   3 packets of 8 beads and 1 packet of 6 beads

5   Joy bought a pair of shorts for $11. Then she bought a scarf for $3. Joy had $18 left. Which equation could be used to find how much money Joy had to start with, *m*?

Ⓐ $18 - 11 + 3 = m$

Ⓑ $18 + 11 - 3 = m$

Ⓒ $m + 11 + 3 = 18$

Ⓓ $m - 11 - 3 = 18$

6   The graph shows how long Jody studied each week day.

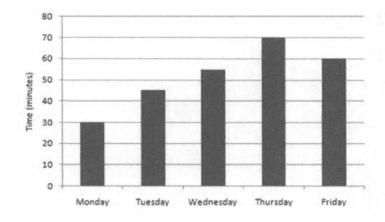

On which day did Jody study for 10 minutes more than the day before?

Ⓐ   Tuesday

Ⓑ   Wednesday

Ⓒ   Thursday

Ⓓ   Friday

7   Davis is making a pictograph to show how many letters three students wrote in a month.

Davis	✉✉✉
Bobby	
Inga	✉✉

Each ✉ means 2 letters.

Bobby wrote 8 letters. How many letter symbols should Davis use to show 8 letters?

Ⓐ   8

Ⓑ   4

Ⓒ   2

Ⓓ   16

8   Bindu is slicing apples into 8 slices. Which table shows how many apple slices Bindu will have if she uses 2, 4, and 5 apples?

Ⓐ

Number of Apples	Number of Slices
2	16
4	32
5	40

Ⓑ

Number of Apples	Number of Slices
2	8
4	32
5	40

Ⓒ

Number of Apples	Number of Slices
2	8
4	32
5	20

Ⓓ

Number of Apples	Number of Slices
2	10
4	20
5	25

9 Look at the number pattern below. If the pattern continues, which two numbers will come next?

$$4, 8, 12, 16, 20, \underline{\quad}, \underline{\quad}$$

Ⓐ   22, 24

Ⓑ   24, 28

Ⓒ   28, 36

Ⓓ   40, 80

10 Which fraction does the shaded model represent?

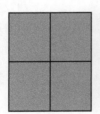  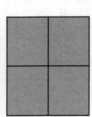 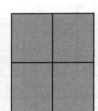 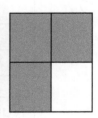

Ⓐ $4\frac{3}{4}$

Ⓑ $4\frac{1}{4}$

Ⓒ $5\frac{3}{4}$

Ⓓ $5\frac{1}{4}$

11 Which fraction model is equivalent to $\frac{1}{2}$?

Ⓐ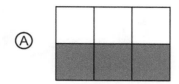

Ⓑ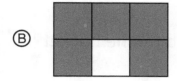

Ⓒ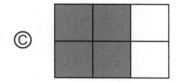

Ⓓ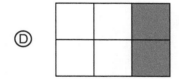

12 Damien folded the shirts and shorts shown below.

What fraction of the clothes folded were shorts?

Ⓐ $\frac{1}{2}$

Ⓑ $\frac{2}{3}$

Ⓒ $\frac{2}{5}$

Ⓓ $\frac{3}{5}$

13 David filled the bucket below with water.

About how much water would it take to fill the bucket?

Ⓐ 5 milliliters

Ⓑ 50 milliliters

Ⓒ 5 liters

Ⓓ 50 liters

14 The Walker family drove 182 miles on Saturday. Then they drove 218 miles on Sunday. How many miles did the family travel in all?

Ⓐ 300 miles

Ⓑ 290 miles

Ⓒ 400 miles

Ⓓ 390 miles

15   Margo sorts apples into 1 kilogram bags to sell. Which of these is most likely to be the number of apples in each bag?

Ⓐ   2 apples

Ⓑ   10 apples

Ⓒ   50 apples

Ⓓ   100 apples

16   A bike ride was held to raise money. There were 70 riders and each rider paid $8 to enter. How much money was raised in all?

Ⓐ $506

Ⓑ $560

Ⓒ $568

Ⓓ $580

17 Sam read 39 pages of a novel in one week. He had 165 pages left to read. How many pages does the novel have?

Ⓐ   204

Ⓑ   136

Ⓒ   194

Ⓓ   126

18 If the numbers below are each rounded to the nearest hundred, which number will be rounded up?

Ⓐ   10,325

Ⓑ   35,682

Ⓒ   23,708

Ⓓ   71,935

19   Leonie has 20 books. She placed an equal number of books on 5 different shelves. There were no books left over.

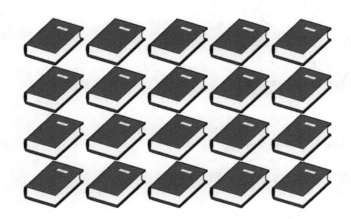

Which number sentence shows how many books Leonie put on each shelf?

Ⓐ   20 + 5 = 25

Ⓑ   20 − 5 = 15

Ⓒ   20 × 5 = 100

Ⓓ   20 ÷ 5 = 4

20 Which of the following has $\frac{1}{3}$ of the stars shaded?

Ⓐ

Ⓑ

Ⓒ

Ⓓ

21   A square garden has side lengths of 8 inches. What is the area of the garden?

Ⓐ   32 square inches

Ⓑ   36 square inches

Ⓒ   48 square inches

Ⓓ   64 square inches

22   Look at the shaded figure below.

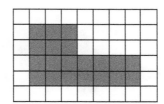

What is the area of the shaded figure?

Ⓐ   20 square units

Ⓑ   22 square units

Ⓒ   26 square units

Ⓓ   28 square units

23 Dannii is training for a bike race. She rode 17 miles on Monday, 19 miles on Tuesday, and 11 miles on Wednesday. Which is the best estimate of how far Dannii rode in all?

Ⓐ   30 miles

Ⓑ   40 miles

Ⓒ   50 miles

Ⓓ   60 miles

24 Squares and rectangles are quadrilaterals. Which of the shapes below is also a quadrilateral?

Ⓐ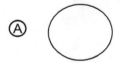

Ⓑ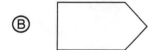

Ⓒ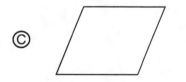

Ⓓ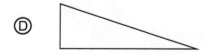

25 The triangle below has a perimeter of 26 cm.

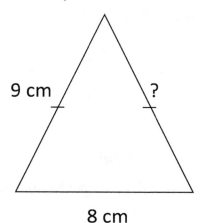

9 cm   ?

8 cm

What is the length of the missing side?

Ⓐ   8 cm

Ⓑ   9 cm

Ⓒ   10 cm

Ⓓ   11 cm

26 The top of a coffee table can be covered completely by 400 square tiles without any gaps or overlaps. If each tile has side lengths of 1 inch, what is the total area of the top of the coffee table?

Ⓐ   100 inches

Ⓑ   400 inches

Ⓒ   100 square inches

Ⓓ   400 square inches

27 Havana is running in a cross country race that goes for 8 miles, as shown on the number line below.

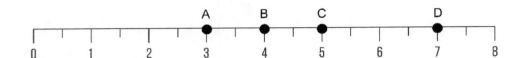

Havana has a water break when she has completed $\frac{5}{8}$ of the race. What point on the number line shows when Havana has a water break?

Ⓐ   Point A

Ⓑ   Point B

Ⓒ   Point C

Ⓓ   Point D

28 Yvonne bought 4 notebooks for $3 each. Then she bought 5 folders for $6 each. Which expression can be used to represent the total amount she spent, in dollars?

Ⓐ $4 + 3 + 5 + 6$

Ⓑ $4 \times 3 \times 5 \times 6$

Ⓒ $(4 \times 3) + (5 \times 6)$

Ⓓ $(4 + 3) \times (5 + 6)$

29 Corey is painting a mural.

  - Corey paints $\frac{1}{8}$ of the mural green.
  - Corey paints $\frac{1}{4}$ of the mural blue.

Which statement shows a correct comparison of the fraction of the mural that is blue and green?

Ⓐ $\frac{1}{8} < \frac{1}{4}$

Ⓑ $\frac{1}{8} > \frac{1}{4}$

Ⓒ $\frac{1}{8} = \frac{1}{4}$

Ⓓ $\frac{1}{8} + \frac{1}{4}$

30 What number makes both equations true?

$$8 \times \underline{\quad} = 32$$
$$32 \div 8 = \underline{\quad}$$

Ⓐ 4

Ⓑ 6

Ⓒ 24

Ⓓ 40

END OF PRACTICE SET

New York Mathematics

Practice Set 7

Short-Response and Extended-Response Questions

Instructions

Read each question carefully. Then write your answer to the question. Be sure to show your work when the question asks you to.

You may use a ruler to help you answer questions. You may not use a calculator on this test.

---

1 One Friday, 5 of a hairdresser's customers were male and 15 were female. What fraction of the hairdresser's customers were male? Write your answer in lowest form. Use the diagram below to help find your answer.

Show your work.

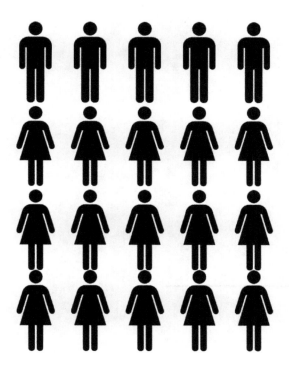

Answer _____ of the customers

2   Which number comes next in the pattern below?

$$4, 8, 16, 32, 64, \underline{\quad}$$

Show your work.

Answer _____

3   Alana finished school at the time shown on the clock below.

Alana arrived home 15 minutes later. What time did Alana arrive home?

Show your work.

Answer _____

4   A box contains 60 cans of soup. Gerald orders 8 boxes of soup for his store. How many cans of soup does Gerald order?

Show your work.

Answer _____ cans of soup

5   Lyn lives 15 miles from her school. Dan lives 3 miles closer than Lyn. How far does Dan live from school?

Show your work.

Answer _____ miles

6   The graph shows the number of points four players scored in a basketball game.

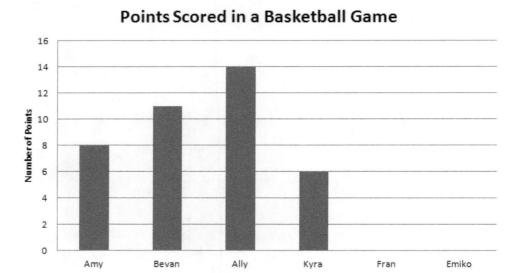

Part A

Fran scored 9 points and Emiko scored 5 points. Add two bars to the graph above to show the points scored by Fran and Emiko.

Part B

How many of the players scored more points than Fran?

Answer _____ players

7   Circle all the shapes below that are quadrilaterals.

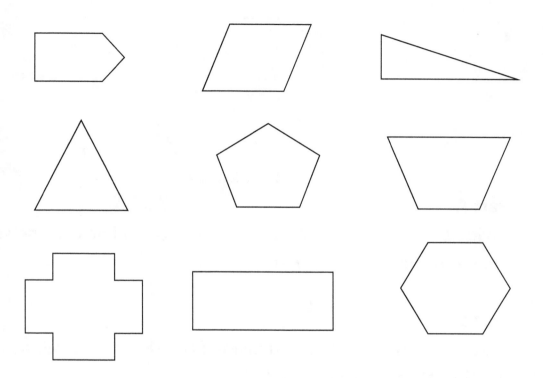

On the lines below, describe the property that is shared by all the shapes you circled.

_____

_____

_____

_____

8   Look at the figure below.

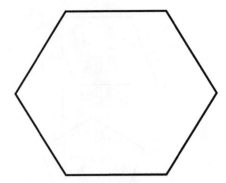

Part A

Divide the shape into 6 equal triangles. Draw lines on the shape above to show your answer.

Part B

Shade 2 of the triangles you divided the shape into. What fraction of the shape is shaded?

Show your work.

Answer _____

9   The top of a rectangular desk is 4 feet long and 3 feet wide.

Part A

What is the area of the top of the desk?

Show your work.

Answer _____

Part B

What is the perimeter of the top of the desk?

Show your work.

Answer _____

10   Look at the shapes below.

Part A

Circle the rhombus.

Part B

On the lines below, describe **two** ways a rhombus is similar to a square.

_____

_____

_____

_____

END OF PRACTICE SET

New York Mathematics

Practice Set 8

Multiple-Choice Questions

Instructions

Read each question carefully. For each multiple-choice question, fill in the circle for the correct answer.

You may use a ruler to help you answer questions. You may not use a calculator on this test.

---

1 What fraction of the letter cards below are vowels?

A E T P S

Ⓐ $\frac{1}{2}$

Ⓑ $\frac{2}{3}$

Ⓒ $\frac{1}{5}$

Ⓓ $\frac{2}{5}$

2 The graph below shows the number of pets four girls have.

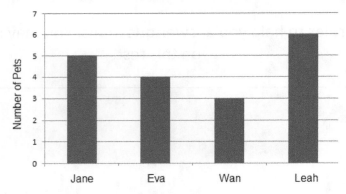

Which two girls have 10 pets in total?

Ⓐ Jane and Eva

Ⓑ Wan and Leah

Ⓒ Eva and Leah

Ⓓ Jane and Wan

3   Rory scored 28 points in a basketball game. Adam scored 4 points less than Rory. Danny scored 6 points more than Adam. How many points did Danny score?

Ⓐ   18

Ⓑ   30

Ⓒ   26

Ⓓ   38

4   Chan had a bag of 27 lollipops. He divided the lollipops evenly between several children.

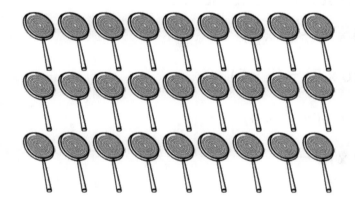

If there were no lollipops left over, how many lollipops could each child have received?

Ⓐ   6

Ⓑ   7

Ⓒ   8

Ⓓ   9

5   Each square on the grid below is 1 cm wide and 1 cm high.

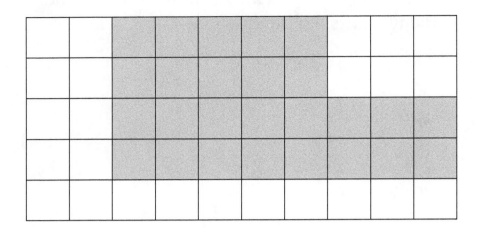

Which expression could be used to find the area of the shaded figure, in square centimeters?

Ⓐ   (5 x 4) + (3 x 2)

Ⓑ   (10 x 5) − (5 x 6)

Ⓒ   (8 x 2) + (5 x 4)

Ⓓ   (8 x 4) − 3

6 Ally bought 3 packets of pencils and 2 packets of pens. There were 8 pencils in each packet, and 6 pens in each packet. Which expression could be used to find how many more pencils she bought than pens?

Ⓐ $(8 \times 6) - (3 \times 2)$

Ⓑ $(8 - 3) \times (6 - 2)$

Ⓒ $(3 \times 8) - (2 \times 6)$

Ⓓ $(3 + 8) - (2 + 6)$

7 Joy is making gift cards. She puts stars on the front of each card. The table shows how many stars she uses for 3, 5, and 6 cards.

Number of Cards	Number of Stars
3	12
5	20
6	24
8	

Based on the table, how many stars would Joy need to make 8 cards?

Ⓐ   28

Ⓑ   32

Ⓒ   36

Ⓓ   26

8   Ling scored 82 on a reading test. Mickey scored 63 on the reading test. Which is the best estimate of how many more points Ling scored than Mickey?

Ⓐ   10

Ⓑ   15

Ⓒ   20

Ⓓ   25

9   The graph below shows the number of different types of trees in an orchard.

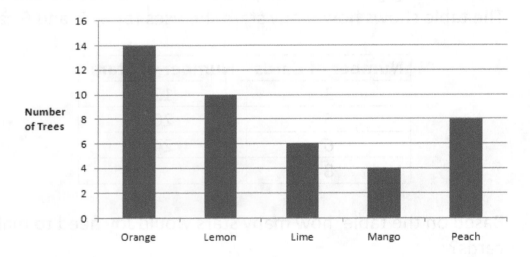

How many more orange trees are there than lime and mango trees combined?

Ⓐ   2

Ⓑ   4

Ⓒ   8

Ⓓ   10

10 A diner has 18 tables. Each table can seat 4 people. The diner also has 8 benches that can each seat 6 people. How many people can the diner seat in all?

Ⓐ   36

Ⓑ   120

Ⓒ   260

Ⓓ   308

11 A rectangle has a length of 6 inches and a height of 5 inches. Which of these shows how to find the perimeter of the rectangle, in inches?

Ⓐ $6 \times 5 = 30$

Ⓑ $6 + 5 = 11$

Ⓒ $2(6 \times 5) = 60$

Ⓓ $2(6 + 5) = 22$

12 Gregory divided a rectangular piece of cardboard into sections, as shown below.

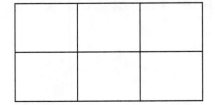

What fraction of the whole is each section?

Ⓐ $\frac{1}{2}$

Ⓑ $\frac{1}{3}$

Ⓒ $\frac{1}{5}$

Ⓓ $\frac{1}{6}$

13 What is the product of 9 and 8?

Ⓐ 56

Ⓑ 64

Ⓒ 72

Ⓓ 81

14 The grade 3 students at Sam's school are collecting cans for a food drive. The table below shows how many cans each class collected.

Class	Number of Cans
Miss Powell	39
Mr. Sato	22
Mrs. Joshi	26
Mr. Perez	37

If each number is rounded to the nearest ten, for which class will the number of cans total 30?

Ⓐ   Miss Powell

Ⓑ   Mr. Sato

Ⓒ   Mrs. Joshi

Ⓓ   Mr. Perez

15 Janine bought a packet of muffins. The packet contained 2 chocolate muffins and 6 vanilla muffins.

What fraction of the muffins were vanilla?

Ⓐ $\frac{1}{3}$

Ⓑ $\frac{1}{4}$

Ⓒ $\frac{1}{6}$

Ⓓ $\frac{1}{8}$

16 What fraction does point *J* represent?

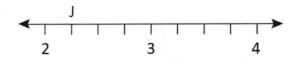

Ⓐ $2\frac{1}{4}$

Ⓑ $2\frac{1}{3}$

Ⓒ $2\frac{1}{5}$

Ⓓ $2\frac{1}{2}$

17 Which number sentence represents the array shown below?

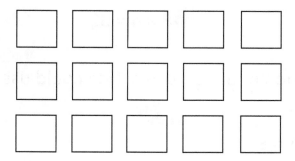

Ⓐ 5 + 3 = 8

Ⓑ 5 × 3 = 15

Ⓒ 15 × 3 = 45

Ⓓ 20 − 5 = 15

18 A pizza has 8 slices. Eriko wants to order enough pizza to have at least 62 slices. What is the least number of pizzas Eriko could order?

Ⓐ 7

Ⓑ 8

Ⓒ 9

Ⓓ 10

19 Tina completes the calculation below.

$$8 \times 4 = 32$$

Which division equation could Tina could use to check her calculation?

Ⓐ $32 \div 4 = 8$

Ⓑ $64 \div 2 = 32$

Ⓒ $8 \div 4 = 2$

Ⓓ $64 \div 8 = 8$

20 What is the most likely mass of the pumpkin below?

Ⓐ   5 grams

Ⓑ   50 grams

Ⓒ   5 kilograms

Ⓓ   50 kilograms

21 Habib measured the length of each wall of his room. A diagram of Habib's room is shown below.

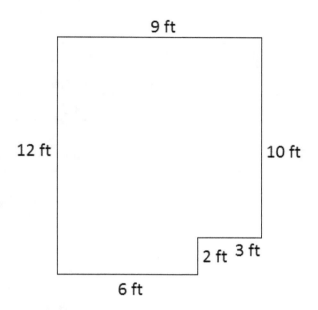

What is the perimeter of Habib's room?

Ⓐ   37 ft

Ⓑ   40 ft

Ⓒ   39 ft

Ⓓ   42 ft

22 Apples are sold in bags. There are the same number of apples in each bag. The table below shows the number of apples in 2, 3, and 4 bags. How many apples are in 6 bags?

Number of Bags	Number of Apples
2	12
3	18
4	24
6	

Ⓐ 30

Ⓑ 28

Ⓒ 36

Ⓓ 42

23 Which shape below is a rectangle?

Ⓐ

Ⓑ

Ⓒ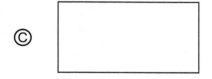

Ⓓ

24   Toni has tokens for arcade games.

If Toni counts her tokens in groups of 6, which list shows only numbers she would count?

Ⓐ   6, 8, 10, 12

Ⓑ   6, 10, 16, 20

Ⓒ   12, 18, 24, 30

Ⓓ   12, 16, 20, 24

25   Which of these is another way of expressing 6 × 14?

Ⓐ   (6 × 10) + (6 × 4)

Ⓑ   (6 × 1) + (6 × 4)

Ⓒ   (6 × 10) + 4

Ⓓ   (6 × 4) + 10

26 Jonathan shades 5 petals of the flower shown below.

What fraction of the petals are shaded?

Ⓐ $\frac{1}{5}$

Ⓑ $\frac{1}{6}$

Ⓒ $\frac{5}{6}$

Ⓓ $\frac{6}{5}$

27 Trevor's baseball team sells 5 packets of tickets to a raffle. Each packet has 60 tickets. What is the total number of raffle tickets sold?

Ⓐ 65

Ⓑ 200

Ⓒ 300

Ⓓ 360

28 Oliver needs 2 cups of flour for a recipe. Oliver only has a measuring cup for $\frac{1}{3}$ cup. How many times would Oliver need to fill the measuring cup to make 2 cups of flour?

Ⓐ 3

Ⓑ 6

Ⓒ 9

Ⓓ 12

29 Which expression represents the situation below?

finding the number of chairs when there are 8 rows of 24 chairs

Ⓐ 24 + 8

Ⓑ 24 − 8

Ⓒ 24 ÷ 8

Ⓓ 24 × 8

30 The shape of a sandpit is shown below.

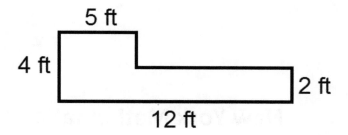

What is the area, in square feet, of the sandpit?

Ⓐ 32

Ⓑ 34

Ⓒ 44

Ⓓ 48

END OF PRACTICE SET

New York Mathematics

Practice Set 9

Multiple-Choice Questions

Instructions

Read each question carefully. For each multiple-choice question, fill in the circle for the correct answer.

You may use a ruler to help you answer questions. You may not use a calculator on this test.

---

1 There are 36 students in a class. The teacher needs to divide the students in the class into teams. Each team must have the same number of students in it. There cannot be any students left over. Which of the following could describe the teams?

Ⓐ   7 teams of 4 students

Ⓑ   9 teams of 4 students

Ⓒ   6 teams of 5 students

Ⓓ   9 teams of 3 students

2 The pictograph shows the emails Sammy sent each week day.

Monday	✉✉✉
Tuesday	✉✉
Wednesday	✉✉✉✉
Thursday	✉✉✉
Friday	✉✉✉✉✉

Each ✉ means 2 emails.

How many emails did Sammy send on Wednesday?

Ⓐ   8

Ⓑ   6

Ⓒ   4

Ⓓ   3

3   What time is shown on the clock below?

Ⓐ   6:30

Ⓑ   7:30

Ⓒ   6:15

Ⓓ   6:45

4   A square garden has side lengths of 8 inches. Jackie makes a rectangular garden with the same area as the square garden. Which of these could be the dimensions of the rectangular garden?

Ⓐ   10 inches by 6 inches

Ⓑ   7 inches by 9 inches

Ⓒ   8 inches by 12 inches

Ⓓ   16 inches by 4 inches

5   Naomi is making a pictograph to show how many fruit trees there are in her yard. The pictograph she has made so far is shown below.

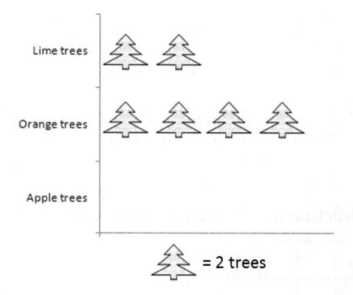

There are 6 apple trees in Naomi's yard. How many tree symbols should Naomi use to show 6 apple trees?

Ⓐ   3

Ⓑ   2

Ⓒ   12

Ⓓ   6

6   Chloe has a 2,000 gram bag of flour. She divides it into smaller bags of 250 grams each. How many smaller bags does she divide the flour into?

Ⓐ   4

Ⓑ   5

Ⓒ   8

Ⓓ   10

7   Which fraction model is equivalent to $\frac{1}{4}$?

Ⓐ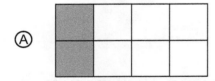

Ⓑ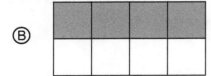

Ⓒ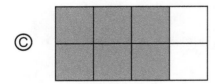

Ⓓ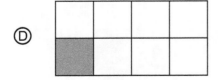

8 A school has 7 school buses. Each bus can seat 48 students. What is the total number of students the buses can seat?

   Ⓐ   266

   Ⓑ   336

   Ⓒ   288

   Ⓓ   284

9 What is the length of the piece of lace shown below?

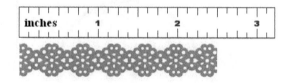

   Ⓐ   2 inches

   Ⓑ $2\frac{1}{2}$ inches

   Ⓒ $2\frac{1}{3}$ inches

   Ⓓ $2\frac{1}{4}$ inches

10 Ribbon costs $4 per yard. Allie has $24 to spend on ribbon. Which equation could be used to find how many yards of ribbon, *y*, she can buy?

Ⓐ $4 \times 24 = y$

Ⓑ $4 \div 24 = y$

Ⓒ $4 \times y = 24$

Ⓓ $4 \div y = 24$

11 Reggie's train leaves at the time shown on the clock below.

What time does Reggie's train leave?

Ⓐ   3:00

Ⓑ   1:15

Ⓒ   1:10

Ⓓ   3:05

12 What do the shaded models below show?

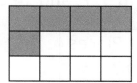 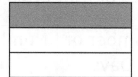

Ⓐ $\frac{5}{12} > \frac{1}{3}$

Ⓑ $\frac{5}{12} = \frac{1}{3}$

Ⓒ $\frac{5}{12} < \frac{4}{12}$

Ⓓ $\frac{5}{7} < \frac{2}{3}$

13 Which number sentence represents the array shown below?

Ⓐ $5 + 4 = 9$

Ⓑ $5 \times 5 = 25$

Ⓒ $5 \times 4 = 20$

Ⓓ $5 - 4 = 1$

14 Lydia eats 2 pieces of fruit every day. Which table shows how many pieces of fruit Lydia eats in 5, 7, and 14 days?

Ⓐ

Number of Days	Number of Pieces of Fruit
5	10
7	14
14	18

Ⓑ

Number of Days	Number of Pieces of Fruit
5	10
7	14
14	20

Ⓒ

Number of Days	Number of Pieces of Fruit
5	10
7	15
14	30

Ⓓ

Number of Days	Number of Pieces of Fruit
5	10
7	14
14	28

15   Melinda buys bagels in packets of 4.

If Melinda counts the bagels in groups of 4, which numbers would she count?

Ⓐ   12

Ⓑ   15

Ⓒ   18

Ⓓ   22

16   Tim scored 21 points in a basketball game. Emmett scored 7 more points than Tim. Which method can be used to find how many points Tim and Emmett scored together?

Ⓐ   Add 21 and 7

Ⓑ   Add 21 to the sum of 21 and 7

Ⓒ   Add 21 to the difference of 21 and 7

Ⓓ   Subtract 7 from 21

17 Which fraction below is the greatest?

Ⓐ $\dfrac{7}{10}$

Ⓑ $\dfrac{4}{5}$

Ⓒ $\dfrac{1}{5}$

Ⓓ $\dfrac{9}{10}$

18 There are 28 students at basketball training. The coach needs to divide the students into groups. Each group must have the same number of students in it. There cannot be any students left over. Which of the following could describe the groups?

Ⓐ 7 groups of 4 students

Ⓑ 8 groups of 3 students

Ⓒ 6 groups of 4 students

Ⓓ 10 groups of 3 students

19 Annie collects baseball cards. She has 22 cards in her collection. She gave her sister 2 baseball cards. Then Annie bought 4 new baseball cards. Which expression can be used to find the number of baseball cards Annie has now?

    Ⓐ   22 + 2 + 4

    Ⓑ   22 + 2 − 4

    Ⓒ   22 − 2 + 4

    Ⓓ   22 − 2 − 4

20 Nate plotted a fraction on the number line below.

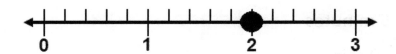

Which fraction could Nate have been plotting?

    Ⓐ $\dfrac{1}{2}$

    Ⓑ $\dfrac{4}{4}$

    Ⓒ $\dfrac{8}{4}$

    Ⓓ $\dfrac{4}{8}$

21 The pictograph below shows how long Tamika spent at the computer each week day.

Monday	🖥🖥🖥🖥
Tuesday	🖥🖥🖥🖥🖥🖥
Wednesday	🖥🖥🖥🖥🖥
Thursday	🖥🖥🖥
Friday	🖥🖥

Each 🖥 means 10 minutes.

How long did Tamika spend at the computer on Wednesday?

Ⓐ   15 minutes

Ⓑ   60 minutes

Ⓒ   5 minutes

Ⓓ   50 minutes

22 A recipe for meatballs calls for $\frac{1}{2}$ teaspoon of cumin. Which fraction is equivalent to $\frac{1}{2}$?

Ⓐ $\frac{2}{6}$

Ⓑ $\frac{2}{4}$

Ⓒ $\frac{4}{6}$

Ⓓ $\frac{3}{2}$

23 Dean drew these shapes.

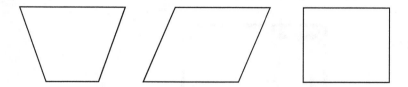

Selma drew these shapes.

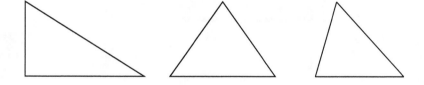

Which shape could be added to Dean's shapes?

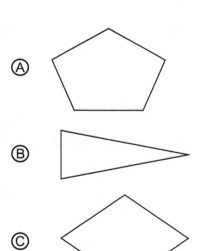

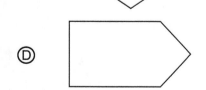

24 A piece of square note paper has side lengths of 5 inches each. What is the perimeter of the note paper?

Ⓐ   10 inches

Ⓑ   20 inches

Ⓒ   25 inches

Ⓓ   30 inches

25 Which measurement is the most likely mass of the apple?

Ⓐ   1 gram

Ⓑ   10 grams

Ⓒ   100 grams

Ⓓ   1,000 grams

26   Cassandra orders 5 water bottles for her office. Each water bottle contains 16 liters of water.

What is the total amount of water in all of the water bottles?

Ⓐ   21 liters

Ⓑ   40 liters

Ⓒ   72 liters

Ⓓ   80 liters

27   A number pattern is shown below.

7, 13, 19, 25, 31, 37

Which rule could have been used to make the pattern?

Ⓐ   Start with 0. Add 6 each time to get the next number.

Ⓑ   Start with 0. Add 7 each time to get the next number.

Ⓒ   Start with 7. Add 6 each time to get the next number.

Ⓓ   Start with 7. Add 7 each time to get the next number.

28   Leonie created four different circle graphs, as shown below.

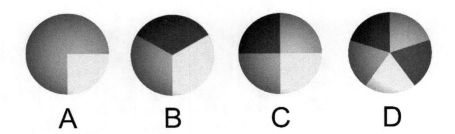

A   B   C   D

Which circle graph is divided into equal thirds?

Ⓐ   Graph A

Ⓑ   Graph B

Ⓒ   Graph C

Ⓓ   Graph D

29 Connor is using the pieces of timber below to make a garden bed.

Which term describes the shape of each face of the timber?

Ⓐ   square

Ⓑ   rectangle

Ⓒ   triangle

Ⓓ   hexagon

30 Which number is represented in the place value diagram below?

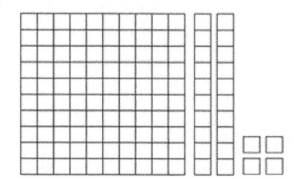

Ⓐ   124

Ⓑ   204

Ⓒ   1,024

Ⓓ   1,204

END OF PRACTICE SET

New York Mathematics

Practice Test 10

Short-Response and Extended-Response Questions

Instructions

Read each question carefully. Then write your answer to the question. Be sure to show your work when the question asks you to.

You may use a ruler to help you answer questions. You may not use a calculator on this test.

1   **Part A**

Plot the number 48 on the number line below.

40   50

Part B

What is the number 48 rounded to the nearest ten?

Answer _____

On the lines below, explain how the number line helped you round the number.

_____

_____

_____

_____

_____

2 Apple trees were planted in rows. Each row had the same number of apple trees.

Number of Rows	Number of Apple Trees
4	24
5	30
6	36
7	42

Based on the table, how many apples trees were in each row?

Show your work.

Answer _____ apple trees

3 Mrs. Anderson took out a loan that will take her 60 months to pay off. How many years will it take Mrs. Anderson to pay off the loan?

1 year = 12 months

Show your work.

Answer _____ years

4   Georgia made the design below.

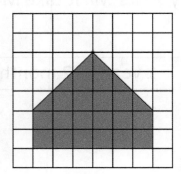

Each square on the grid measures 1 square centimeter. What is the area of the shaded part of the design?

Show your work.

Answer _____ square centimeters

5   The table below shows how many customers a restaurant had on each day of the week.

Day	Number of Customers
Monday	28
Tuesday	21
Wednesday	36
Thursday	32
Friday	45

How many more customers did the restaurant have on Friday than on Monday?

Show your work.

Answer _____ customers

6   The table below shows Emma's savings over four months.

Month	Amount Saved ($)
Jan	18
Feb	16
Mar	14
Apr	19

Part A

Complete the graph below using the data in the table.

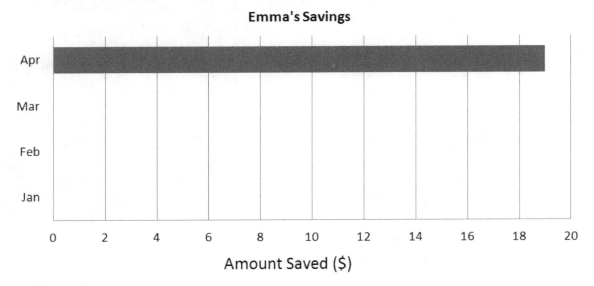

Part B

What is the difference between the most and the least she saved each month?

Show your work.

Answer _____

7   Look at the number pattern below.

$$7, 10, 13, 16, 19, 22, \underline{\quad\quad}$$

If the pattern continues, which number will come next?

Answer _____

On the lines below, explain how you found your answer.

_____

_____

_____

_____

_____

8   The picture below represents a playground.

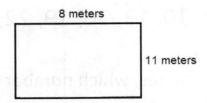

8 meters

11 meters

A fence is being built to go around the edge of the playground. The timber for the fence costs $14 per meter. If enough timber is bought to fit exactly around the edge of the playground, how much will the timber cost?

Show your work.

Answer _____

9 During a golf game, Gia scored below par on 3 of the 18 holes.

Part A

Divide the rectangle below into segments and shade the rectangle to show what fraction of the holes Gia scored below par on.

Part B

What fraction of the holes did Gia score below par on? Write your answer in lowest form.

Show your work.

Answer _____

10 What are the two smallest 3-digit numbers that can be made using the digits 1, 6, and 4? Each digit must be used only once in each number.

Answer _____ and _____

On the lines below, explain how you found your answer.

_____

_____

_____

_____

_____

END OF PRACTICE SET

ANSWER KEY

Mathematics Learning Standards

In 2017, the state of New York introduced the Next Generation Learning Standards. These are revised standards that replace the previous Common Core Learning Standards, though remain very close in content. Beginning with the 2020/2021 school year, the state tests will assess the Next Generation Learning Standards. This workbook has aligned all questions to the new Next Generation Learning Standards.

Assessing Skills and Knowledge

The skills listed in the Next Generation Learning Standards are divided into five topics, or domains. These are:

- Operations and Algebraic Thinking
- Number and Operations in Base Ten
- Number and Operations – Fractions
- Measurement and Data
- Geometry

The answer key identifies the topic for each question. Use the topics listed to identify general areas of strength and weakness. Then target revision and instruction accordingly.

The answer key also identifies the specific math skill that each question is testing. Use the skills listed to identify skills that the student is lacking. Then target revision and instruction accordingly.

Scoring Short-Response and Extended-Response Questions

This practice test book includes short-response and extended-response questions, where students provide a written answer to a question or complete a task. These questions are often scored based on the final answer given as well as the work shown. When asked to show work, students may show calculations, use diagrams, or explain their thinking or process in words. Any form of work that shows the student's understanding can be accepted. Other questions are scored based on tasks completed, explanations given, or justifications given. Answers are provided for these questions, as well as guidance on how to score the questions.

New York Mathematics, Practice Set 1

Question	Answer	Topic	Next Generation Learning Standard
1	B	Number & Operations-Fractions	Understand a fraction as a number on the number line; represent fractions on a number line.
2	B	Measurement & Data	Tell and write time to the nearest minute and measure time intervals in minutes. Solve one-step word problems involving addition and subtraction of time intervals in minutes.
3	A	Measurement & Data	Measure and estimate liquid volumes and masses of objects using standard units of grams (g), kilograms (kg), and liters (l).
4	(4 × 8) + 5 37	Operations/Algebraic Thinking	Solve two-step word problems using the four operations. Represent these problems using equations or expressions with a letter standing for the unknown quantity.
5	1st, 3rd, 5th, and 6th	Operations/Algebraic Thinking	Fluently solve single-digit multiplication and related divisions, using strategies such as the relationship between multiplication and division or properties of operations.
6	See Below	Number & Operations-Fractions	Understand a fraction as a number on the number line; represent fractions on a number line. Express whole numbers as fractions, and recognize fractions that are equivalent to whole numbers.
7	See Below	Measurement & Data	Draw a scaled bar graph to represent a data set with several categories.
8	See Below	Geometry	Recognize and classify polygons based on the number of sides and vertices (triangles, quadrilaterals, pentagons, and hexagons). Identify shapes that do not belong to one of the given subcategories.
9	See Below	Measurement & Data	Find areas of rectilinear figures by decomposing them into non-overlapping rectangles and adding the areas of the non-overlapping parts. Solve real world and mathematical problems involving perimeters of polygons, including finding the perimeter given the side lengths.
10	See Below	Measurement & Data	Identify rectangles with the same perimeter and different areas or with the same area and different perimeters.

Q6.
The numbers should be plotted as below.

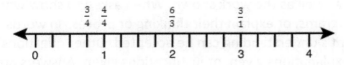

Scoring Information
Give a total score out of 2.
Give a score of 0.5 for each number correctly plotted.

Q7.
The graph should be completed with a bar to 12 for Action, a bar to 14 for Comedy, and a bar to 8 for Drama.

Scoring Information
Give a total score out of 3.
Give a score of 1 for each bar correctly added.

Q8.
The student should circle the trapezoid.
The student should explain that the trapezoid does not have two pairs of parallel sides or that the trapezoid only has one pair of parallel sides. The answer should show an understanding that parallelograms have two pairs of parallel sides.

Scoring Information
Give a total score out of 3.
Give a score of 1 for circling the trapezoid.
Give a score out of 2 for the explanation.

Q9.
The student should complete the missing dimensions of 2 ft and 11 ft.
The student may divide the shape into a 3 by 7 rectangle and a 2 by 8 rectangle or a 3 by 5 rectangle and an 11 by 2 rectangle.
The student should find an area of 37 square feet.
The student should find a perimeter of 36 feet.

Scoring Information
Give a total score out of 3.
Give a score of 0.5 for each correct missing dimension.
Give a score of 1 for dividing the shape correctly.
Give a score of 0.5 for the correct area.
Give a score of 0.5 for the correct perimeter.

Q10.
The student should draw a 6 by 2 rectangle on the grid.
The student should explain that the second rectangle has an area of 12 square units, but a perimeter of 14 units. The answer should show an understanding that rectangles with the same area do not always have the same perimeter.

Scoring Information
Give a total score out of 3.
Give a score of 1 for drawing a correct rectangle.
Give a score out of 2 for the explanation.

New York Mathematics, Practice Set 2

Question	Answer	Topic	Next Generation Learning Standard
1	C	Number & Operations in Base Ten	Fluently add and subtract within 1,000 using strategies and algorithms.
2	5, 10, 15, 20, 25	Operations/Algebraic Thinking	Identify and extend arithmetic patterns.
3	B	Measurement & Data	Tell and write time to the nearest minute and measure time intervals in minutes.
4	$1\frac{1}{4}$ inches or 1.25 inches	Measurement & Data	Generate measurement data by measuring lengths using rulers marked with halves and fourths of an inch.
5	2nd, 3rd, and 4th	Number & Operations-Fractions	Recognize and generate equivalent fractions. Explain why the fractions are equivalent.
6	C	Operations/Algebraic Thinking	Use multiplication and division within 100 to solve word problems in situations involving equal groups, arrays, and measurement quantities.
7	$717	Number & Operations in Base Ten	Fluently add and subtract within 1,000 using strategies and algorithms.
8	See Below	Operations/Algebraic Thinking	Identify and extend arithmetic patterns.
9	See Below	Measurement & Data	Draw a scaled bar graph to represent a data set with several categories. Solve one- and two-step "how many more" and "how many less" problems using information presented in scaled bar graphs.
10	See Below	Measurement & Data	Recognize area as additive. Find areas of figures composed of non-overlapping rectangles, and apply this technique to solve real world problems.

Q8.
26, 30, 34, 38
The student should identify that all the numbers will be even. The student should explain that all the numbers will be even because an even number is always being added to an even number.

Scoring Information
Give a total score out of 3.
Give a score of 0.5 for each correct number in the pattern.
Give a score of 1 for identifying that all the numbers will be even and explaining why.

Q9.
Friday
40 minutes
30 minutes

Scoring Information
Give a total score out of 3.
Give a score of 1 for each correct answer.

Q10.
Rectangle 1: 2 by 4 units   Rectangle 2: 2 by 6 units
Area: 20 square units

Scoring Information
Give a total score out of 3.
Give a score of 1 for each correct answer.

New York Mathematics, Practice Set 3

Question	Answer	Topic	Next Generation Learning Standard
1	B	Operations/Algebraic Thinking	Interpret products of whole numbers.
2	Wednesday	Measurement & Data	Solve one- and two-step "how many more" and "how many less" problems using information presented in scaled bar graphs.
3	D	Number & Operations-Fractions	Express whole numbers as fractions, and recognize fractions that are equivalent to whole numbers.
4	B	Measurement & Data	Draw a scaled picture graph to represent a data set with several categories.
5	B	Operations/Algebraic Thinking	Solve two-step word problems posed with whole numbers and having whole-number answers using the four operations.
6	C	Operations/Algebraic Thinking	Represent problems using equations or expressions with a letter standing for the unknown quantity.
7	25,600	Number & Operations in Base Ten	Use place value understanding to round whole numbers to the nearest 10 or 100.
8	A	Operations/Algebraic Thinking	Assess the reasonableness of answers using mental computation and estimation strategies including rounding.
9	A	Number & Operations in Base Ten	Fluently add and subtract within 1,000 using strategies and algorithms based on place value, properties of operations, and/or the relationship between addition and subtraction.
10	Point at $1\frac{1}{4}$	Number & Operations-Fractions	Understand a fraction as a number on the number line; represent fractions on a number line.
11	See Below	Number & Operations in Base Ten	Use place value understanding to round whole numbers to the nearest 10 or 100.
12	See Below	Number & Operations-Fractions	Understand a unit fraction, $1/b$, is the quantity formed by 1 part when a whole is partitioned into b equal parts.
13	See Below	Number & Operations-Fractions	Compare two fractions with the same numerator or the same denominator by reasoning about their size. Record the results of comparisons with the symbols >, =, or <, and justify the conclusions.
14	See Below	Operations/Algebraic Thinking	Identify and extend arithmetic patterns.
15	See Below	Operations/Algebraic Thinking	Apply properties of operations as strategies to multiply and divide.
16	C	Number & Operations in Base Ten	Multiply one-digit whole numbers by multiples of 10 in the range 10–90 using strategies based on place value and properties of operations.
17	30 – 6 + 2 = 26	Operations/Algebraic Thinking	Solve two-step word problems using the four operations. Represent these problems using equations or expressions with a letter standing for the unknown quantity.
18	A	Number & Operations in Base Ten	Understand that the digits of a four-digit number represent amounts of thousands, hundreds, tens, and ones.
19	D	Number & Operations-Fractions	Understand a unit fraction, $1/b$, is the quantity formed by 1 part when a whole is partitioned into b equal parts.
20	D	Measurement & Data	Tell and write time to the nearest minute and measure time intervals in minutes.

Q11.
110, 90, 280, 980, 860, 200, 40, 770
The student should provide an explanation that refers to considering the number in the ones place. The answer should include that the number is rounded down if the number is less than 5 and rounded up if the number is 5 or higher.

Scoring Information
Give a total score out of 3.
Give a score of 0.25 for each number correctly rounded.
Give a score out of 1 for the explanation.

Q12.
$$\frac{5}{19}$$
The work should show winning 5 games out of a total of 5 + 14 = 19 games.

Scoring Information
Give a total score out of 2.
Give a score of 1 for the correct answer.
Give a score out of 1 for the working.

Q13.
The two models should have shaded 3 of the 10 segments and 2 of the 10 segments.
The > symbol should be placed in the empty box.
The student may explain how shading the models allows the two fractions to be compared by seeing how many parts of 10 each fraction is. The student may explain how you can compare the fractions as parts of the same whole.

Scoring Information
Give a total score out of 3.
Give a score of 1 for each correct shading.
Give a score of 1 for the correct symbol.
Give a score out of 1 for the explanation.

Q14.
Expression: $x + 3$
Answer: 34
Answer: 115

Scoring Information
Give a total score out of 3.
Give a score of 1 for the correct expression.
Give a score of 1 for each correct answer.

Q15.
6 × 5 = 30, then 30 × 3 = 90 OR 5 × 6 = 30, then 30 × 3 = 90
6 × 3 = 18, then 18 × 5 = 90 OR 3 × 6 = 18, then 18 × 5 = 90
5 × 3 = 15, then 15 × 6 = 90 OR 3 × 5 = 15, then 15 × 6 = 90

Scoring Information
Give a total score out of 3.
Give a score of 1 for each correct number sentence.

New York Mathematics, Practice Set 4

Question	Answer	Topic	Next Generation Learning Standard
1	A	Geometry	Partition shapes into parts with equal areas. Express the area of each part as a unit fraction of the whole.
2	A	Operations/Algebraic Thinking	Understand division as an unknown-factor problem.
3	B	Measurement & Data	Recognize a plane figure which can be covered without gaps or overlaps by *n* unit squares is said to have an area of *n* square units.
4	A	Geometry	Recognize and classify polygons based on the number of sides and vertices (triangles, quadrilaterals, pentagons, and hexagons). Identify shapes that do not belong to one of the given subcategories.
5	B	Measurement & Data	Measure and estimate masses of objects.
6	D	Operations/Algebraic Thinking	Identify and extend arithmetic patterns.
7	16 cans	Measurement & Data	Draw a scaled picture graph to represent a data set with several categories.
8	C	Measurement & Data	Solve real world and mathematical problems involving perimeters of polygons, including finding the perimeter given the side lengths.
9	75, 90, 105	Operations/Algebraic Thinking	Identify and extend arithmetic patterns.
10	C	Number & Operations-Fractions	Understand a fraction *a/b* as the quantity formed by *a* parts of size 1/*b*.
11	See Below	Number & Operations in Base Ten	Use place value understanding to round whole numbers to the nearest 10 or 100.
12	See Below	Operations/Algebraic Thinking	Use multiplication and division within 100 to solve word problems in situations involving equal groups, arrays, and measurement quantities.
13	See Below	Measurement & Data	Tell and write time to the nearest minute and measure time intervals in minutes. Solve one-step word problems involving addition and subtraction of time intervals in minutes.
14	See Below	Number & Operations-Fractions	Recognize and generate equivalent fractions. Explain why the fractions are equivalent.
15	See Below	Measurement & Data	Identify rectangles with the same perimeter and different areas or with the same area and different perimeters.
16	B	Measurement & Data	Draw a scaled picture graph to represent a data set with several categories.
17	D	Operations/Algebraic Thinking	Solve two-step word problems posed with whole numbers and having whole-number answers using the four operations.
18	$575	Number & Operations in Base Ten	Fluently add and subtract within 1,000 using strategies and algorithms based on place value, properties of operations, and/or the relationship between addition and subtraction.
19	B	Operations/Algebraic Thinking	Fluently solve single-digit multiplication and related divisions, using strategies such as the relationship between multiplication and division or properties of operations.
20	A	Measurement & Data	Identify rectangles with the same perimeter and different areas or with the same area and different perimeters.

Q11.
Nearest ten: 8,780
Nearest hundred: 8,800
The student should provide an explanation that refers to considering the number in the ones place when rounding to the nearest ten and considering the number in the tens place when rounding to the nearest hundred. The answer should include that the number is rounded down if the number is less than 5 and rounded up if the number is 5 or higher.

Scoring Information
Give a total score out of 3.
Give a score of 1 for each correct rounding.
Give a score out of 1 for the explanation.

Q12.
$6
The work may show the division calculation 96 ÷ 16 = 6. The work could use the missing factor equation 16 × s = 96.

Scoring Information
Give a total score out of 2.
Give a score of 1 for the correct answer.
Give a score out of 1 for the working.

Q13.
91 minutes
The work may show calculating 25 minutes to 2 p.m., 60 minutes to 3 p.m., and 6 minutes to 3:06 p.m., and finding the sum of 25, 60, and 6. The work may show calculating 120 minutes from 1:35 to 3:35 and then subtracting (35 – 6) from 120. The work may show calculating 120 minutes from 3:06 to 1:06 and then subtracting (35 – 6) from 120. Other ways of calculating the elapsed time may also be accepted.

Scoring Information
Give a total score out of 2.
Give a score of 1 for the correct answer.
Give a score out of 1 for the working.

Q14.
The halves fraction bar should have 1 of the 2 segments shaded.
The quarters fraction bar should have 2 of the 4 segments shaded.
The eighths fraction bar should have 4 of the 8 segments shaded.
Fraction: $\frac{4}{8}$

Scoring Information
Give a total score out of 2.
Give a score of 0.5 for each fraction bar correctly shaded.
Give a score of 0.5 for the correct fraction.

Q15.
18 square units
The grid should have a 6 by 3 rectangle drawn on it.

Scoring Information
Give a total score out of 3.
Give a score of 1 for the correct area.
Give a score of 2 for a 6 by 3 rectangle.
Give a score of 1 for a non-rectangular shape with an area of 18 square units.

New York Mathematics, Practice Set 5

Question	Answer	Topic	Next Generation Learning Standard
1	C	Measurement & Data	Recognize perimeter as an attribute of plane figures and distinguish between linear and area measures.
2	D	Measurement & Data	Multiply side lengths to find areas of rectangles with whole-number side lengths in the context of solving real world and mathematical problems.
3	A	Operations/Algebraic Thinking	Solve two-step word problems posed with whole numbers and having whole-number answers using the four operations.
4	D	Number & Operations in Base Ten	Use place value understanding to round whole numbers to the nearest 10 or 100.
5	C	Operations/Algebraic Thinking	Interpret whole-number quotients of whole numbers.
6	A	Operations/Algebraic Thinking	Solve two-step word problems posed with whole numbers and having whole-number answers using the four operations.
7	A	Measurement & Data	Recognize area as an attribute of plane figures and understand concepts of area measurement, including that a plane figure which can be covered without gaps or overlaps by n unit squares is said to have an area of n square units.
8	C	Operations/Algebraic Thinking	Assess the reasonableness of answers using mental computation and estimation strategies including rounding.
9	C	Operations/Algebraic Thinking	Interpret products of whole numbers and whole-number quotients of whole numbers.
10	A	Operations/Algebraic Thinking	Determine the unknown whole number in a multiplication or division equation relating three whole numbers.
11	A	Measurement & Data	Solve one- and two-step "how many more" and "how many less" problems using information presented in scaled bar graphs.
12	B	Measurement & Data	Recognize area as an attribute of plane figures and understand concepts of area measurement, including that a plane figure which can be covered without gaps or overlaps by n unit squares is said to have an area of n square units.
13	B	Number & Operations in Base Ten	Use place value understanding to round whole numbers to the nearest 10 or 100.
14	B	Number & Operations-Fractions	Recognize and generate equivalent fractions. Explain why the fractions are equivalent.
15	C	Operations/Algebraic Thinking	Interpret products of whole numbers.
16	D	Number & Operations-Fractions	Understand a fraction as a number on the number line; represent fractions on a number line.
17	A	Number & Operations-Fractions	Understand a unit fraction, $1/b$, is the quantity formed by 1 part when a whole is partitioned into b equal parts. Understand a fraction a/b as the quantity formed by a parts of size $1/b$.
18	A	Operations/Algebraic Thinking	Use multiplication and division within 100 to solve word problems in situations involving equal groups, arrays, and measurement quantities.
19	C	Number & Operations-Fractions	Compare two fractions with the same numerator or the same denominator by reasoning about their size.

20	B	Measurement & Data	Solve real world and mathematical problems involving perimeters of polygons.
21	A	Geometry	Partition shapes into parts with equal areas.
22	D	Operations/Algebraic Thinking	Apply properties of operations as strategies to multiply and divide.
23	C	Operations/Algebraic Thinking	Identify and extend arithmetic patterns.
24	C	Measurement & Data	Multiply side lengths to find areas of rectangles with whole-number side lengths in the context of solving real world and mathematical problems.
25	A	Operations/Algebraic Thinking	Represent problems using equations or expressions with a letter standing for the unknown quantity.
26	C	Measurement & Data	Solve one-step word problems involving addition and subtraction of time intervals in minutes.
27	B	Operations/Algebraic Thinking	Apply properties of operations as strategies to multiply and divide.
28	C	Operations/Algebraic Thinking	Fluently solve single-digit multiplication and related divisions, using strategies such as the relationship between multiplication and division or properties of operations.
29	C	Measurement & Data	Add, subtract, multiply, or divide to solve one-step word problems involving masses or liquid volumes that are given in the same units.
30	D	Number & Operations in Base Ten	Use place value understanding to round whole numbers to the nearest 10 or 100.

New York Mathematics, Practice Set 6

Question	Answer	Topic	Next Generation Learning Standard
1	D	Operations/Algebraic Thinking	Solve two-step word problems posed with whole numbers and having whole-number answers using the four operations.
2	B	Measurement & Data	Solve one- and two-step "how many more" and "how many less" problems using information presented in scaled bar graphs.
3	C	Number & Operations-Fractions	Recognize and generate equivalent fractions. Explain why the fractions are equivalent.
4	D	Operations/Algebraic Thinking	Use multiplication and division within 100 to solve word problems in situations involving equal groups, arrays, and measurement quantities.
5	D	Operations/Algebraic Thinking	Represent problems using equations or expressions with a letter standing for the unknown quantity.
6	B	Measurement & Data	Solve one- and two-step "how many more" and "how many less" problems using information presented in scaled bar graphs.
7	B	Measurement & Data	Draw a scaled picture graph to represent a data set with several categories.
8	A	Operations/Algebraic Thinking	Use multiplication and division within 100 to solve word problems in situations involving equal groups, arrays, and measurement quantities.
9	B	Operations/Algebraic Thinking	Identify and extend arithmetic patterns.
10	A	Number & Operations-Fractions	Understand a unit fraction, $1/b$, is the quantity formed by 1 part when a whole is partitioned into b equal parts. Understand a fraction a/b as the quantity formed by a parts of size $1/b$.
11	A	Number & Operations-Fractions	Recognize and generate equivalent fractions. Explain why the fractions are equivalent.
12	C	Number & Operations-Fractions	Understand a unit fraction, $1/b$, is the quantity formed by 1 part when a whole is partitioned into b equal parts.
13	C	Measurement & Data	Measure and estimate liquid volumes.
14	C	Number & Operations in Base Ten	Fluently add and subtract within 1,000 using strategies and algorithms.
15	B	Measurement & Data	Measure and estimate liquid volumes and masses of objects using standard units of grams (g), kilograms (kg), and liters (l). Add, subtract, multiply, or divide to solve one-step word problems involving masses or volumes that are given in the same units.
16	B	Number & Operations in Base Ten	Multiply one-digit whole numbers by multiples of 10 in the range 10–90 using strategies based on place value and properties of operations.
17	A	Number & Operations in Base Ten	Fluently add and subtract within 1,000 using strategies and algorithms based on place value, properties of operations, and/or the relationship between addition and subtraction.
18	B	Number & Operations in Base Ten	Use place value understanding to round whole numbers to the nearest 10 or 100.

19	D	Operations/Algebraic Thinking	Interpret whole-number quotients of whole numbers.
20	D	Number & Operations-Fractions	Understand a unit fraction, $1/b$, is the quantity formed by 1 part when a whole is partitioned into b equal parts. Understand a fraction a/b as the quantity formed by a parts of size $1/b$.
21	D	Measurement & Data	Multiply side lengths to find areas of rectangles with whole-number side lengths in the context of solving real world and mathematical problems.
22	A	Measurement & Data	Recognize area as additive. Find areas of figures composed of non-overlapping rectangles, and apply this technique to solve real world problems.
23	C	Operations/Algebraic Thinking	Assess the reasonableness of answers using mental computation and estimation strategies including rounding.
24	C	Geometry	Recognize and classify polygons based on the number of sides and vertices (triangles, quadrilaterals, pentagons, and hexagons). Identify shapes that do not belong to one of the given subcategories.
25	B	Measurement & Data	Solve real world and mathematical problems involving perimeters of polygons, including finding one unknown side length given the perimeter and other side lengths.
26	D	Measurement & Data	Find the area of a rectangle with whole-number side lengths by tiling it, and show that the area is the same as would be found by multiplying the side lengths.
27	C	Number & Operations-Fractions	Understand a fraction as a number on the number line; represent fractions on a number line.
28	C	Operations/Algebraic Thinking	Solve two-step word problems posed with whole numbers and having whole-number answers using the four operations.
29	A	Number & Operations-Fractions	Compare two fractions with the same numerator or the same denominator by reasoning about their size.
30	A	Operations/Algebraic Thinking	Apply properties of operations as strategies to multiply and divide.

New York Mathematics, Practice Set 7

Question	Points	Topic	Next Generation Learning Standard
1	2	Number & Operations-Fractions	Understand a unit fraction, $1/b$, is the quantity formed by 1 part when a whole is partitioned into b equal parts. Understand a fraction a/b as the quantity formed by a parts of size $1/b$.
2	2	Operations/Algebraic Thinking	Identify and extend arithmetic patterns.
3	2	Measurement & Data	Tell and write time to the nearest minute and measure time intervals in minutes. Solve one-step word problems involving addition and subtraction of time intervals in minutes.
4	2	Number & Operations in Base Ten	Multiply one-digit whole numbers by multiples of 10 in the range 10–90 using strategies based on place value and properties of operations.
5	2	Number & Operations in Base Ten	Fluently add and subtract within 1,000 using strategies and algorithms based on place value, properties of operations, and/or the relationship between addition and subtraction.
6	3	Measurement & Data	Draw a scaled bar graph to represent a data set with several categories. Solve one- and two-step "how many more" and "how many less" problems using information presented in scaled bar graphs.
7	3	Geometry	Recognize and classify polygons based on the number of sides and vertices (triangles, quadrilaterals, pentagons, and hexagons). Identify shapes that do not belong to one of the given subcategories.
8	3	Geometry	Partition shapes into parts with equal areas. Express the area of each part as a unit fraction of the whole.
9	3	Measurement & Data	Solve real world and mathematical problems involving areas and perimeters of rectangles.
10	3	Geometry	Recognize and classify polygons based on the number of sides and vertices (triangles, quadrilaterals, pentagons, and hexagons). Identify shapes that do not belong to one of the given subcategories.

Q1.

$\frac{1}{4}$ of the customers

The work should use the diagram to show that 1 out of 4 customers were male.

Scoring Information

Give a total score out of 2.

Give a score of 1 for the correct answer. Give a score of 0.5 if the fraction $\frac{5}{20}$ is given.

Give a score out of 1 for the working.

Q2.

128

The work should show that the student understands that each number in the pattern is twice the one before it.

Scoring Information

Give a total score out of 2.

Give a score of 1 for the correct answer.

Give a score out of 1 for the working.

Q3.
3:45
The work should show that the clock shows 3:30, and then add 15 minutes to this time.

Scoring Information
Give a total score out of 2.
Give a score of 1 for the correct answer.
Give a score out of 1 for the working.

Q4.
480 cans of soup
The work should show the calculation of 60 × 8 = 480. The work may show the calculation of 6 × 8 = 48, and then the addition of a zero to the end of the number to give 480.

Scoring Information
Give a total score out of 2.
Give a score of 1 for the correct answer.
Give a score out of 1 for the working.

Q5.
12 miles
The work should show the calculation of 15 − 3 = 12.

Scoring Information
Give a total score out of 2.
Give a score of 1 for the correct answer.
Give a score out of 1 for the working.

Q6.
Part A
The student should add a bar to 9 for Fran and a bar to 5 for Emiko.

Part B
2 players

Scoring Information
Give a total score out of 3.
Give a score of 1 for each bar correctly added in Part A.
Give a score of 1 for the correct answer in Part B.

Q7.
The rhombus, the trapezoid, and the rectangle should be circled.
The property identified could be that all the shapes have four sides or that all the shapes have four angles.

Scoring Information
Give a total score out of 3.
Give a score of 2 if the three shapes are correctly circled.
Give a score of 1 if only 1 or 2 of the shapes are correctly circled, or if additional shapes are also circled.
Give a score out of 1 for the explanation.

Q8.
Part A
The student should divide the hexagon into 6 equal triangles, as shown below.

Part B
$\frac{1}{3}$ or $\frac{2}{6}$

Scoring Information
Give a total score out of 3.
Give a score of 1 for a correct division into 6 triangles in Part A.
Give a score of 1 for the correct answer in Part B.
Give a score out of 1 for the working in Part B.

Q9.
Part A
12 square feet
The work could show the calculation $4 \times 3 = 12$, or could use a diagram of a 4 by 3 rectangle.

Part B
14 feet
The work should show the calculation $4 + 4 + 3 + 3 = 14$ or $(2 \times 4) + (2 \times 3) = 14$.

Scoring Information
Give a total score out of 3.
Give a score of 1 for the correct answer to Part A.
Give a score of 1 for the correct answer to Part B.
Give a score out of 1 for the working.

Q10.
Part A
The rhombus in the center should be circled.

Part B
Answers may describe any two of the following similarities:
- They both have 4 sides or 4 equal sides.
- They both have 4 angles.
- They both have congruent or equal sides.
- They both have parallel sides.

Scoring Information
Give a total score out of 3.
Give a score of 1 for the correct shape circled.
Give a score of 1 for each similarity correctly described.

New York Mathematics, Practice Set 8

Question	Answer	Topic	Next Generation Learning Standard
1	D	Number & Operations-Fractions	Understand a unit fraction, 1/b, is the quantity formed by 1 part when a whole is partitioned into b equal parts. Understand a fraction a/b as the quantity formed by a parts of size 1/b.
2	C	Measurement & Data	Solve one- and two-step "how many more" and "how many less" problems using information presented in scaled bar graphs.
3	B	Operations/Algebraic Thinking	Solve two-step word problems posed with whole numbers and having whole-number answers using the four operations.
4	D	Operations/Algebraic Thinking	Interpret whole-number quotients of whole numbers.
5	A	Measurement & Data	Recognize area as additive. Find areas of figures composed of non-overlapping rectangles, and apply this technique to solve real world problems.
6	C	Operations/Algebraic Thinking	Solve two-step word problems posed with whole numbers and having whole-number answers using the four operations.
7	B	Operations/Algebraic Thinking	Identify and extend arithmetic patterns.
8	C	Operations/Algebraic Thinking	Assess the reasonableness of answers using mental computation and estimation strategies including rounding.
9	B	Measurement & Data	Solve one- and two-step "how many more" and "how many less" problems using information presented in scaled bar graphs.
10	B	Operations/Algebraic Thinking	Solve two-step word problems posed with whole numbers and having whole-number answers using the four operations.
11	D	Measurement & Data	Solve real world and mathematical problems involving perimeters of polygons, including finding the perimeter given the side lengths.
12	D	Geometry	Partition shapes into parts with equal areas. Express the area of each part as a unit fraction of the whole.
13	C	Operations/Algebraic Thinking	Know from memory all products of two one-digit numbers.
14	C	Number & Operations in Base Ten	Use place value understanding to round whole numbers to the nearest 10 or 100.
15	B	Number & Operations-Fractions	Recognize and generate equivalent fractions. Explain why the fractions are equivalent.
16	A	Number & Operations-Fractions	Understand a fraction as a number on the number line; represent fractions on a number line.
17	B	Operations/Algebraic Thinking	Interpret products of whole numbers.
18	B	Operations/Algebraic Thinking	Use multiplication and division within 100 to solve word problems in situations involving equal groups, arrays, and measurement quantities.

19	A	Operations/Algebraic Thinking	Fluently solve single-digit multiplication and related divisions, using strategies such as the relationship between multiplication and division or properties of operations.
20	C	Measurement & Data	Measure and estimate masses of objects.
21	D	Measurement & Data	Solve real world and mathematical problems involving perimeters of polygons, including finding the perimeter given the side lengths.
22	C	Operations/Algebraic Thinking	Identify and extend arithmetic patterns.
23	C	Geometry	Recognize and classify polygons based on the number of sides and vertices (triangles, quadrilaterals, pentagons, and hexagons). Identify shapes that do not belong to one of the given subcategories.
24	C	Operations/Algebraic Thinking	Identify and extend arithmetic patterns.
25	A	Operations/Algebraic Thinking	Apply properties of operations as strategies to multiply and divide.
26	C	Number & Operations-Fractions	Understand a fraction a/b as the quantity formed by a parts of size $1/b$.
27	C	Number & Operations in Base Ten	Multiply one-digit whole numbers by multiples of 10 in the range 10-90 using strategies based on place value and properties of operations.
28	B	Number & Operations-Fractions	Express whole numbers as fractions, and recognize fractions that are equivalent to whole numbers.
29	D	Operations/Algebraic Thinking	Represent problems using equations or expressions with a letter standing for the unknown quantity.
30	B	Measurement & Data	Recognize area as additive. Find areas of figures composed of non-overlapping rectangles, and apply this technique to solve real world problems.

New York Mathematics, Practice Set 9

Question	Answer	Topic	Next Generation Learning Standard
1	B	Operations/Algebraic Thinking	Use multiplication and division within 100 to solve word problems in situations involving equal groups, arrays, and measurement quantities.
2	A	Measurement & Data	Draw a scaled picture graph to represent a data set with several categories.
3	B	Measurement & Data	Tell and write time to the nearest minute and measure time intervals in minutes.
4	D	Measurement & Data	Multiply side lengths to find areas of rectangles with whole-number side lengths in the context of solving real world and mathematical problems.
5	A	Measurement & Data	Draw a scaled picture graph to represent a data set with several categories.
6	C	Measurement & Data	Add, subtract, multiply, or divide to solve one-step word problems involving masses or volumes that are given in the same units.
7	A	Number & Operations-Fractions	Recognize and generate equivalent fractions. Explain why the fractions are equivalent.
8	B	Operations/Algebraic Thinking	Solve two-step word problems posed with whole numbers and having whole-number answers using the four operations.
9	B	Measurement & Data	Generate measurement data by measuring lengths using rulers marked with halves and fourths of an inch.
10	C	Operations/Algebraic Thinking	Understand division as an unknown-factor problem.
11	B	Measurement & Data	Tell and write time to the nearest minute and measure time intervals in minutes.
12	A	Number & Operations-Fractions	Record the results of comparisons with the symbols >, =, or <, and justify the conclusions.
13	C	Operations/Algebraic Thinking	Interpret products of whole numbers.
14	D	Operations/Algebraic Thinking	Use multiplication and division within 100 to solve word problems in situations involving equal groups, arrays, and measurement quantities.
15	A	Operations/Algebraic Thinking	Interpret products of whole numbers.
16	B	Operations/Algebraic Thinking	Solve two-step word problems posed with whole numbers and having whole-number answers using the four operations.
17	D	Number & Operations-Fractions	Compare two fractions with the same numerator or the same denominator by reasoning about their size.
18	A	Operations/Algebraic Thinking	Use multiplication and division within 100 to solve word problems in situations involving equal groups, arrays, and measurement quantities.
19	C	Operations/Algebraic Thinking	Solve two-step word problems posed with whole numbers and having whole-number answers using the four operations.
20	C	Number & Operations-Fractions	Express whole numbers as fractions, and recognize fractions that are equivalent to whole numbers.
21	D	Measurement & Data	Draw a scaled picture graph to represent a data set with several categories.
22	B	Number & Operations-Fractions	Recognize and generate equivalent fractions.

23	C	Geometry	Recognize and classify polygons based on the number of sides and vertices (triangles, quadrilaterals, pentagons, and hexagons). Identify shapes that do not belong to one of the given subcategories.
24	B	Measurement & Data	Solve real world and mathematical problems involving perimeters of polygons, including finding the perimeter given the side lengths.
25	C	Measurement & Data	Measure and estimate masses of objects.
26	D	Measurement & Data	Add, subtract, multiply, or divide to solve one-step word problems involving masses or liquid volumes that are given in the same units.
27	C	Operations/Algebraic Thinking	Identify and extend arithmetic patterns.
28	B	Number & Operations-Fractions	Understand a unit fraction, $1/b$, is the quantity formed by 1 part when a whole is partitioned into b equal parts.
29	B	Geometry	Recognize and classify polygons based on the number of sides and vertices (triangles, quadrilaterals, pentagons, and hexagons). Identify shapes that do not belong to one of the given subcategories.
30	A	Number & Operations in Base Ten	Read and write four digit numbers using base-ten numerals, number names, and expanded form.

New York Mathematics, Practice Set 10

Question	Points	Topic	Next Generation Learning Standard
1	3	Number & Operations in Base Ten	Use place value understanding to round whole numbers to the nearest 10 or 100.
2	2	Operations/Algebraic Thinking	Identify and extend arithmetic patterns.
3	2	Operations/Algebraic Thinking	Use multiplication and division within 100 to solve word problems in situations involving equal groups, arrays, and measurement quantities.
4	2	Measurement & Data	Recognize area as an attribute of plane figures and understand concepts of area measurement, including that a plane figure which can be covered without gaps or overlaps by n unit squares is said to have an area of n square units.
5	2	Number & Operations in Base Ten	Fluently add and subtract within 1,000 using strategies and algorithms based on place value, properties of operations, and/or the relationship between addition and subtraction.
6	3	Measurement & Data	Draw a scaled bar graph to represent a data set with several categories. Solve one- and two-step "how many more" and "how many less" problems using information presented in scaled bar graphs.
7	3	Operations/Algebraic Thinking	Identify and extend arithmetic patterns.
8	3	Measurement & Data	Solve real world and mathematical problems involving perimeters of polygons, including finding the perimeter given the side lengths.
9	3	Number & Operations-Fractions	Recognize and generate equivalent fractions. Explain why the fractions are equivalent.
10	2	Number & Operations in Base Ten	Understand that the digits of a four-digit number represent amounts of thousands, hundreds, tens, and ones.

Q1.
Part A
The number 48 should be plotted on the number line.

Part B
50

The student should explain how you can tell that the number is closer to 50 than 40.

Scoring Information
Give a total score out of 3.
Give a score of 1 for the number correctly plotted in Part A.
Give a score of 1 for the correct answer in Part B.
Give a score out of 1 for the explanation.

Q2.
6 apple trees
The work may show a division calculation such as 24 ÷ 4 or 30 ÷ 5. The work may also indicate that for every 1 more row added, there are another 6 apple trees.

Scoring Information
Give a total score out of 2.
Give a score of 1 for the correct answer.
Give a score out of 1 for the working.

Q3.
5 years
The work should show the calculation of 60 ÷ 12 = 5 or 12 + 12 + 12 + 12 + 12 = 60.

Scoring Information
Give a total score out of 2.
Give a score of 1 for the correct answer.
Give a score out of 1 for the working.

Q4.
21 square centimeters
The work should show that the student counted the number of squares. The work could show counting the number of whole squares and then the number of half squares. The work could involve dividing the shape into a rectangle and a triangle or a rectangle and two triangles. The work could also involve recognizing that the two triangles combine to form a 3 by 3 square.

Scoring Information
Give a total score out of 2.
Give a score of 1 for the correct answer.
Give a score out of 1 for the working.

Q5.
17
The work should show the calculation of 45 − 28 = 17.

Scoring Information
Give a total score out of 2.
Give a score of 1 for the correct answer.
Give a score out of 1 for the working.

Q6.
Part A
The student should add a bar to 18 for Jan, a bar to 16 for Feb, and a bar to 14 for Mar.

Part B
$5

The work could show the calculation of 19 − 14 = 5. or could use the graph to find the difference between the two bars.

Scoring Information
Give a total score out of 3.
Give a score of 0.5 for each bar correctly added in Part A.
Give a score of 1 for the correct answer in Part B.
Give a score of 0.5 for the working in Part B.

Q7.
25
The explanation should describe how each number in the pattern is 3 more than the number before it, and that the next number is found by adding 3 to 22.

Scoring Information
Give a total score out of 3.
Give a score of 1 for the correct answer.
Give a score out of 2 for the explanation.

Q8.
$532
The work should show the calculation of the perimeter as 8 + 8 + 11 + 11 = 38 meters.
The work should show the calculation of the timber cost as 38 × 14 = 532.

Scoring Information
Give a total score out of 3.
Give a score of 1 for the correct perimeter found.
Give a score of 1 for the correct cost found.
Give a score out of 1 for the working.

Q9.
Part A
The model should have 3 parts of 18 shaded, or 1 part of 6 shaded, as shown below.

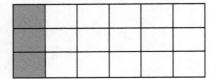 or

Part B
$\frac{1}{6}$
The student may simplify $\frac{3}{18}$ to $\frac{1}{6}$. The student may also refer to using the model to determine the fraction, such as by explaining that 1 part of 6 total parts is shaded.

Scoring Information
Give a total score out of 3.
Give a score of 1 for the correct shading in Part A.
Give a score of 1 for the correct answer in Part B.
Give a score out of 1 for the working in Part B.

Q10.
146 and 164
The explanation should refer to the place value of the numbers. It may describe how the number with the lowest value should be in the hundreds place.

Scoring Information
Give a total score out of 2.
Give a score of 0.5 for each correct number.
Give a score out of 1 for the explanation.

Printed in the USA
CPSIA information can be obtained
at www.ICGtesting.com
LVHW081413240823
756072LV00007B/588